D0627758

The World's Creepiest Places

GHP

Dr. Bob Curran

Illustrations by Ian Daniels

New Page Books
A Division of
The Career Press
Pompton Plains, NJ

THE WORLD'S CREEPIEST PLACES
EDITED AND TYPESET BY GINA TALUCCI
Cover and interior art by Ian Daniels
Printed in the U.S.A.

To order this title, please call toll-free 1-800-CAREER-1 (NJ and Canada: 201-848-0310) to order using VISA or MasterCard, or for further information on books from Career Press.

The Career Press, Inc.
220 West Parkway, Unit 12
Pompton Plains, NJ 07444
www.careerpress.com
www.newpagebooks.com

Library of Congress Cataloging-in-Publication Data

Curran, Bob.
    The world's creepiest places / by Bob Curran ; illustrations by Ian Daniels.
          p. cm.
    Includes bibliographical references and index.
    ISBN 978-1-60163-190-9 -- ISBN 978-1-60163-636-2 (ebook) 1. Haunted places. I. Daniels, Ian. II. Title.

BF1461.C87 2012
133.109--dc23
                                                              2011027035

Contents

Introduction

"I want to make your flesh creep."
—The fat boy in *The Pickwick Papers* by Charles Dickens

What makes our flesh crawl? What is it that gives the sensation of cold fingers running up and down our spines or of the hairs on the back of our necks prickling and rising? And why would such sensations be associated with certain places and localities?

The dictionary defines the word *creepy* as "an unusual or unpleasant sensation of uneasiness or fear as of things crawling or creeping on one's skin." Probably we have all experienced such feelings at one time or another—when we are alone and uncertain, when we are in an unfamiliar or perhaps threatening place, when we are faced with the unusual or frightening. "Creepiness" then is a basic response to where we are or what is going on around us, to the unfamiliar or to what we *imagine* might happen to us. And perhaps it is our ability to respond in both mental and physical terms that holds the key. What if we were to see a ghost, what if we were to feel its touch? If we shiver at these words, then it is both our imaginary and our physical senses that are responding. We can envisage what it might be like. Similarly, with some person who is odd or strange or who has unfamiliar ways about them—the unkempt old man who seems to be following you down the road; the old woman who talks to herself on the bus or subway; the person who "just doesn't look right" whom you meet on the street; or a neighbor who might behave differently or oddly on a fairly regular basis—we sometimes describe such people as "creepy." Once again, this constitutes a response (usually instantaneous) to something which we've encountered. Our fears or uncertainties about what such people might be or do are manifesting themselves in a physical way. But what about a building or a specific place?

A good number of years ago, I temporarily worked in Belfast and rented a flat in what had once been a relatively prosperous residential area, but which was now in a kind of genteel decline. Each morning, as I walked down to catch the bus into the city, I had to pass, at the very end of the tree-lined street where I lived, a large house that stood at its very end and where my street met a main road. The building stood in its own grounds, well back from the road, and was surrounded by a tall and rather unkempt hedge. The entrance to it was a rusty iron gate, which had obviously not been opened in a long time, and which was secured with a chain and a padlock. It was a solid four-square house, old fashioned but large and imposing in its own way—a sloping ornamented roof and large wood-framed windows. I could imagine that it was the sort of house that would have once been the home of a fairly wealthy and respectable family. Clearly, no one lived there now, for large and heavy main doors were permanently closed and the garden beyond was an absolute tangle into which all manner of rubbish—empty beer cans and paper bags mainly—had been thrown. A couple of the windows had been boarded up and several more were adorned with heavy old-fashioned shutters; two or three peered down almost malevolently on all who passed too close to the rusting gate. The paint and plaster were peeling and an air of forlorn decay hung about the entire dwelling, but this also seemed to give it an air of menace. Each time I passed it on my way to and from the bus stop, I felt a little bit uneasy, as though the house itself were somehow *aware* of me and followed me as I walked in front of the rusty gate with an unfriendly eye. And as I walked up the street to my flat, I felt the odd and unpleasant sensation all through my body. Sometimes as I passed by, I thought that I glimpsed something or someone at an uncurtained window or disappearing around the corner of a falling wooden garage at the side, but it was probably no more than my own imagination.

On one occasion I spoke to my landlady (who lived in the same house as myself) about the house at the end of the street, asking her almost casually if she knew anything about it. She knew nothing (she had only lived in the area for a few years) except that it had always been empty. However, she thought that she had heard that something very nasty had happened there many years before—a murder perhaps, maybe even of a child—but she couldn't be sure. She, too, admitted that every time she passed by it she always experienced a certain unpleasant feeling—it gave her "the creeps." From then on, the house took on an even more sinister aspect, and I actually found myself increasing my step as I walked past the rusting gateway. Sometimes as I passed by, I was almost sure that I heard the cry of a child from somewhere close by, and I remembered what the landlady had said about the supposed murder. I imagined that somebody stood at the window in one of those musty rooms to watch me go past and that he or she meant me (or anybody) no good. The feeling that I'd had about the old place seemed to grow stronger—"the creeps" more intense. However, my work in Belfast finished and I moved away and the house at the end of the street was lost in memory. But the feelings about it somehow remained, and I still would remember it from time to time with a slight shudder.

Not so long ago, I had reason to go back to the area; I drove my car along the busy road and passed the end of the street where I once lived. On an impulse I turned my car into it and stopped. The house was still there, but it was very different. It was certainly the same building, but it was now a bright, modernized, family home. The tangled lawn had been cut and tidied, and there were childrens' toys—a swing and a slide and some bouncy things. The doors and windows had been painted, the stonework had been re-pointed and re-plastered, and a modern garage had been built at the side. A new gate lay open and welcoming. And as I stood there, I realized that there were no "creepy" feelings associated with the place at all. I later asked a man from the area about the house and if there was a history attached to it. He said that he'd never heard anything even vaguely sinister about it—it had been owned at one time by an old couple who had no children and who had let it get "badly run down." When they had died, the place had passed through the hands of various people, none of whom had actually lived there, and fell further into decay until it was bought and modernized. When I asked about the supposed murder, he shook his head. He'd never heard of any murder connected with the house, let alone the murder of a child or of anything particularly nasty happening there. "The house looked so dilapidated," he said, "that I suppose people started to make up stories about it. But there was nothing to them."

I thought about the house at the end of the street (and several other old houses that I've known) when I was asked to write this book. In fact, as it came into my mind, I experienced once again that tingling through my body as I had all those years ago. What is it that makes a place "creepy" and can give us the distinct sensation that I experienced when I passed by that rusty gate? What is it that made it stay in my memory through the years? Maybe some of you know of similar places—maybe even at the end of your own street—that make you feel "uncomfortable." It doesn't actually have to be a house though, or even a street—perhaps it's a particular spot way out in the country or in a woodland or an abandoned factory, but most people that I've talked to know of some place that gives them an odd or strange feeling, or gives them a sensation as if their skin were crawling. But what are the essentials of "creepiness"? Thinking about my own experiences, I might venture to make a few suggestions.

The first is that the very appearance of the place provoked an adverse response in me as I passed it. The other houses on the street were inhabited and were usually bright and cheerful with obvious signs of activity all around them. The house at the end of the street, however, was gloomy, decayed, and menacing-looking, the sort of appearance that might be associated with unsavoury activity or with the occult or the supernatural. It was not hard to imagine that it had been the site of some murder or that it was haunted. Just as with the dishevelled woman, talking animatedly to herself and smelling of drink, we all too readily seek for references and make assumptions around what we see. The woman may pester us for money or she might be mad and try to do us harm in some way—or so we think. Our reaction to her is therefore determined by the references and preconceptions that we carry with us and by our own imagination. And it is the same with a house or a place. We don't usually feel "creepy" in a bright, spacious, modern family home (though in some fictional stories this has sometimes been the case), but the mental and emotional references associated with some old building, dilapidated and sinister looking, lend themselves to such a feeling. Some places genuinely give off an aura of menace and threat whether that is justified or not. And it is here that our imaginations take over—we *expect* that place to be haunted or for some bizarre or unusual event to occur there, and this forms the basis of our response to such a location. When I walked past the house on my way to and from work, for instance, I had the distinct impression that someone or *something* watched me from one of the dusty, unshuttered, upper windows. In the back of my mind, I imagined something moving through the unfurnished rooms of the building, waiting for someone to come up to the door to investigate. There was, of course, probably nothing but damp and must in the place. And yet, the very appearance of the house triggered such an impression in me. And I do not appear to have been alone in this respect as my discussion with the landlady verified. Sinister woodlands, lonely forest glades and paths, lonely roads, and gloomy hills also all carry the same sort of aura about them and have the power to provoke such reaction. Sometimes there is no real reason for this. In the countryside where I grew up, there were many abandoned houses, cottages, and barns, set away in inaccessible places that, as a child, I only viewed from a distance. And yet there was a sense of menace about them. Distant stone walls set among gloomy trees often took on a slightly sinister atmosphere in the late afternoon sun and seemed a place where evil might indeed dwell. It would, perhaps, be very unwise to venture there, for who knew what I might see within their precincts? "If that house isn't haunted" an old man in County Waterford once told me, "then it should be!" Such is the power of the imagination and of impression.

A second, and not unconnected, suggestion regarding the "creepiness" of the site lies in the history or traditions of the place itself. A place where a battle has occurred, a prison where inmates have been maltreated, or a site where a brutal murder has taken place are bound to have associations that can stir up reactions within us. Maybe it is down to the idea that strong and often violent emotions have been released—emotions with which many of us can empathise. Similarly, in a place where we hear of strong emotions such as unrequited or frustrated love, we can sometimes experience the same feelings. Tales of a doomed lover, an abandoned bride, or a lost child, all can provoke some sort of reaction that we might describe as "the creeps." What if these powerful events can leave some sort of emotive imprint on the site where they occurred, and what if we can somehow gain access to this? Is this what we mean by a "ghost" or by a supernatural experience?

But it is not only places where great or spectacular events have occurred that can provoke such response. Areas in which perhaps smaller dramas have taken place do so too, to a greater or lesser extent. A room in a house, a stretch of roadway, or a yard or a field where something unusual has taken place can be just as "creepy."

When I was much younger, I can recall a great house that stood about 2 miles from where my grandmother lived. My grandfather had worked there as a laborer for a while, and it was owned by an unmarried man; the last of his family who lived there with a housekeeper to look after him. Although I always imagined that he had a great deal of money, in hindsight, I suspect that he didn't have all that much—certainly not enough to maintain the house which he had allowed to run down. To a child it was a ghostly place, dark and musty with long corridors that seemed to lead nowhere, and damp and moldy rooms off of them where no fires had been lit. Here mildewed family photos hung on the walls looking down on faded furniture and dust. Although it has featured in one way or another in some of my writing, it didn't frighten me all that much; except for one room. There was an old story that one of the landlord's brothers, who was blind, had gone mad, and in the way of genteel families in Ireland long ago, was kept locked up in one of the rooms on the top floor where the maids had formerly slept. He had died there in that narrow room, but his sightless ghost still haunted the room, fumbling and scraping its way around on the other side of a locked door. The floor was accessed by a sweep of the main staircase, but because there were now no maids, no one really ever went up there. But I found the sweep of the stairs and the upper story a terrifying place, and, even in my early teens, I experienced a "creepy sensation" every time I was up there. Once as a little boy, I'd gone to the very top of the staircase and had stood outside the door of the "haunted room," hearing something shuffle and move on the other side of the closed door. Upon reflection it might have been no more than birds that had managed to get in through broken slates in the roof moving about in an otherwise empty room, but to a small child, it was almost certainly something ghostly and with frightening intent. I ran down the staircase, below those frowning, heavily framed photos on the walls, convinced that something mad and blind was following me, reaching out to grab me, and the thrill of absolute terror was tingling all over me. Even writing about it years later, I can still get a sense of that creepy feeling stealing along my spine. Of course, the housekeeper completely dismissed the idea of a ghost in the room when I eventually told her, but I noticed that she kept well away from the upper floor herself. She told me that it was because the floors in the rooms up there were rotten and dangerous—hadn't one of my uncles fallen through the floor and broken his leg? However, I think that she also had the same creepy feeling that I had experienced up there—for all her talk she was a very superstitious woman. The associations in the room, whether real or imagined, seemed to completely permeate the entire upper stories of that old house.

And something of that same sensation filled me when I passed the house at the end of the street, many years later, especially when I thought that a child might have been murdered there. All the references that I had about the place came into play. At night I thought that I saw a light move from window to window (it might well have been a reflection of the street light) and the nearby cry of a bird or a fox suddenly became the wail of an infant. And I had the impression that somebody somehow came through the gate and followed me up the road toward my own house. Of course when I turned around, there was nothing or no one there. But the sensation remained. I still imagined that *something* from the shadowy house dogged my footsteps home.

And perhaps imagination may well be the key to our response. The appearance of a place, coupled perhaps with some notion of its history, triggers our imagination, and we can visualize some horror or threat waiting to confront us. That is what perhaps excites the feeling of creepiness. Before he fell through the rotten floorboards, my uncle—a solid, no-nonsense man—had worked on the ghostly upper floor of the gloomy old house for the best part of a week and, as far as I know, experienced nothing. He admitted the place was dilapidated, badly lit, and claustrophobic, and he knew the supposed story about the ghostly closed room. However, he maybe didn't have the imagination to turn those references into the "creepy feeling." So maybe creepiness is a combination of things drawing together into a specific reaction.

At least that's the explanation that I give you as a psychologist and a philosopher. But what if I'm wrong? What if, despite all the psychological and perhaps glib suggestions, we do possess an innate ability to recognize the supernatural or the encroaching forces of another world? What if the house at the end of the street *was* haunted by something unpleasant from its past? My friend who told me about the area readily admitted that he didn't know *all* of its history, only the more recent stuff. What if some time way back in the past, a child *had* been murdered there? People can forget, but not old houses.

So whether you are a skeptic or a believer, whether you want to understand more or just want to be plain scared, come with us now and visit some genuinely creepy places all across the world. They cover a wide variety of locations and experiences, and though you may dismiss at least some of them, remember: For many of us there is always some place like the house at the end of the street lurking somewhere at the back of our minds.

Bachelor's Grove

Chicago, Illinois

"The glow-worm o'er grave and stone,
Shall light thee steady,
The owl from the steeple sing,
'Welcome proud lady.'"
—Sir Walter Scott, "Proud Maisie" from *Heart of Midlothian*

The old burial ground at Bachelor's Grove Cemetery, set out in Chicago's Rubio Woods between the Midlothian Turnpike and the Oak Forest is certainly one of America's spookiest graveyards. Badly overgrown, filled with fallen trees and tangled vegetation, the old place exudes an air of mystery and decay that can often unsettle even the most stout-hearted visitor.

Even the name of the ancient cemetery and when it was initially opened is something of a mystery. Some people confidently state that the name "Bachelor's Grove" derives from the number of unmarried men who lie buried within its precincts. Others state that it comes from a local family named Bachelor who owned the land before the cemetery opened its gates.

Nor can anybody agree as to when the place first became a graveyard, although many suggest that it was around the 1840s. They point out that the earliest stones within the place seem to date from around 1844. Recently, however, a local paper noted a tombstone erected to a William Nobles, which was dated 1838, and it is possible that there are even older ones on site. The first formally recorded burial in the site was that of Eliza Scott (wife of Leonard H. Scott) in November 1844, but local newspapers suggest that there may have been others that were slightly older.

The settlement of Bachelor's Grove seems to date from around the 1820s with an influx of English, Irish, and Scottish settlers often referred to as "the First Wave," most of whom came from New York, Vermont, and Connecticut. These people seem to have formed a small but thriving settlement about 18 miles southwest of Chicago. The "Second Wave," which was mainly Germanic, arrived sometime about the late 1840s and quickly became the predominant nationality in the area. Among these German immigrants there appears to have been a family named Bechelder who took lands in Cook County and helped enlarge the settlement. So is Bachelor's Grove really Bechelder's Grove as *A Gazetteer of Illinois* (published in 1832) would seem to indicate? This would perhaps also explain the differences in the spelling of the name of the cemetery—sometimes "Bachelor's" (conventional English) and at other times "Batchelor's" (which may lend itself more to the German original).

Although there are clearly tombstones in the old graveyard dating from around 1840, the first formal record of the cemetery occurs in 1864 when Edward M. Everden sold a parcel of land to Frederick Schmidt with the proviso that a portion of it—approximately one acre—be set aside for a graveyard. Schmidt did so, and, at some point, allegedly added a further area to the original plot, although records in a local newspaper give no evidence for this, but suggest that there may have been a cemetery there beforehand. What Schmidt *may* have acquired was a small lake that was a pool from a small quarry nearby, which still lies within the cemetery grounds. The cemetery was run by a board of trustees, made up of local families, among which were the Fulton family, who seem to have arrived in the area around 1844.

The way down to the burial ground from the Midlothian Turnpike was quiet and secluded and it became a favored area for lovers and courting couples, but, if rumours are to be believed, for other things as well. Among some of the German immigrants there were tales of devil worship, brought from areas such as the Brocken and the Hartz Mountain country. Some of the Germans had brought pagan beliefs from the Old World, some of which involved dead bodies, and these were still practiced in secluded, out-of-the-way places, such as the Bachelor's Grove cemetery. Of course, many of these rumors and tales may have had their origins in personal disputes and feuds amongst the various waves of settlers, but they served to give the place a rather sinister reputation. The isolation of the cemetery too must have also had an impact upon the imaginations of local people, for as long as there have been records concerning it, the place was believed to be haunted, perhaps by spirits that have been summoned up in secret.

The trail that led down to the cemetery was a spooky place. It was part of the Midlothian Turnpike, which was closed to traffic in the early 1960s to make way for a new street (143rd Street), with the road being formally closed in 1977; this has isolated the cemetery even more. It is alleged that the road work stirred up the ghosts in the old graveyard even more. Ghostly stories concerning the site grew and spread through Chicago and beyond, as did the stories of Satanism and devil worship within its precincts. There was no doubt that both sightseers, followers of the macabre, and vandals visited the place, each leaving their mark as they came and went. Even chaining off the road didn't help and the vandals often found ways around, leaving all sorts of litter across the old graveyard and desecrating many of the graves that were there (perhaps for ritualistic purposes). In order to maintain some measure of control, the Civic Authorities appointed a watchman, Charlie Fulton (a descendant of one of the old settler families who had graves there—his Christian name is also given as Clarence) to oversee the place. Charlie, who retired in the mid-1970s, seems to have been quite a character who wrote several pieces for various local newspapers about the cemetery. In the early days of the 20th century, he said, the graveyard was a place for picnicking families who would come to enjoy the tranquillity of the place and occasionally to swim in the nearby pond. By contrast, however, many of his tales were ghost stories and concerned the specters which he claimed to see on his rounds as a watchman after dark. He (and a number of others since) claimed to hear strange voices calling in the twilight and saw strange figures moving among the funeral markers, even in broad daylight. One of the most famous phantoms, as recounted by Charlie, is that of the White Lady, also known as "the Madonna of Bachelor's Grove" or more affectionately as "Mrs. Rodgers" who wandered the cemetery each night, sometimes with an infant in her arms, peering at many of the other headstones. One old story says that she is the restless spirit of a mother who died and was buried alongside her infant during one of the great epidemics that hit the Chicago area in the late 19th century. She returned each night to restlessly wander through the cemetery, perhaps looking for the child's father who may have died at a later date and was buried separately. She seems lost in a forlorn world of her own and is totally unaware of the people whom she might pass.

Although the White Lady is a phantom, a curious photo, taken of the Madonna of Bachelor's Grove does exist. Intrigued by reports of balls of light (many mentioned by Charlie Fulton) and of glowing ectoplasmic strands adhered to trees and bushes within the parameters of the graveyard, the Ghost Research Society decided to investigate the site. One of the researchers, Mari Huff, took a photo of what she claimed was an empty space between several tombstones using high-speed infra-red equipment. When the photo was developed, however, it showed the figure of a woman sitting on a tombstone, seemingly in a reflective mood. Parts of her body appeared to be transparent and her dress seemed to be that of a former time. The photo remains one of the most celebrated and most mysterious images of a ghost available.

During the Gangster Era in Chicago, the isolation of Bachelor's Grove allegedly played its part in the city's turbulent history. It is reputed that several Chicago gang bosses had victims taken out to this lonely spot in order to have them executed. Their bodies were then dumped in the lake. One of the most notorious of the gang leaders was the famous Al Capone. It is said that several of Capone's victims lie buried in unmarked graves somewhere around the very edge of the pond, which is now covered in algae. No one will go hunting for their resting places today! Along the narrow track that leads down to the cemetery, the headlights of phantom cars have often been seen, suggestive of this era and the mobsters who brought their hapless prisoners down to Bachelor's Grove in order to meet their end.

Of course, the large pond has something of a spectral history. The most common story it tells is of a man who was ploughing with his horse at the end of the 19th century. Something startled the animal and it bolted into the water. The farmer's foot got caught in the fastenings of the plough and he was dragged along with it, unable to free himself in time. Both the man and animal drowned. However, both their ghosts are supposed to haunt the immediate area of the pond. In the 1970s, two rangers of the Cook County Forest Preserve were a patrolling the area close to the pond when suddenly out of the water a great horse rose up. The animal seemed to be pulling a plough, which was steered by an old man who also emerged from the pond. These apparitions made their way across in front of the

rangers' vehicle and vanished into the surrounding woodlands. The two men sat dumbfounded, unsure of what they had seen, but knowing that it was certainly not of this world. Did it prove the legend of the drowned farmer? The area in which the vision was seen is strongly associated with "light orbs," small globes of light that seem to signal the presence of spirits, which appear to drift along the edges of the pond.

The final apparition involves an entire ghostly house that has been appearing and disappearing for several decades. There is no formal record of a house, although local traditions state that Frederick Schmidt may have built a timber-frame house there just before he originally extended the land that enclosed the graveyard. Most of the reports concerning this phantom come from people who believe that they have seen an actual house and descriptions of it seldom vary. It is an old two-story timber-frame house with a front porch and a light shining in the window as if to welcome the stranger in. Sometimes the door appears to be slightly ajar, but the story is that if you enter the building, you will never come out again—at least not in this world. The house appears at all times—day or night—and in all weathers. As ever, all along the narrow pathway, eerie globes of light flicker as if to show the passing of otherworldly things.

And the rumours of Satanic festivals and actual grave desecrations haven't gone away. In fact, the situation is so bad that the Cook County Sheriff's Office had now imposed a curfew, arresting those who are found around the location at night. Special patrols now operate in the area around Halloween and those arrested are charged with trespass and possible intent to commit an offense. This is clearly an attempt to keep youths away from the site, but it still does not deter some members of the public from venturing close. As late as the 1990s, people have described what appear to be figures in monkish habits coming and going around the entrance of the old burial ground, and somewhere near the gates, a couple of visitors claim to have seen a large black dog that disappeared as soon as they approached it. In 2007, a television crew for the popular show *Cringe* visited the cemetery along with the well-known ghost hunter Troy Taylor. According to Taylor, from the moment they began to set up their equipment, things went wrong. In the course of the filming, digital footage was inexplicably distorted and destroyed, which was something that no member of the crew had ever encountered before. There was also an attempt to record a podcast that had to be abandoned because of unexplained distortions in the sound combined with odd noises and equipment failures. It was something that shook the whole crew.

The final stretch of road leading past the cemetery was closed in 1994 and the lane that leads to it has been cordoned off. Few appear to travel there now as according to local reports instances of vandalism have died down. The dead now rest easy in Bachelor's Grove. Or do they?

Cabell's Tomb

Buckfastleigh, England

"Mr Holmes, they were the footprints of a gigantic hound!"
—Sir Arthur Conan Doyle, *The Hound of the Baskervilles*

Even on the most pleasant day, Dartmoor can be an eerie place. Miles of rolling bog and moorland dotted with the tombs of prehistoric men, with small villages tucked away in misty hollows, all serve to stimulate either romance—or fear—in most of us. And the eerie character of the place manifests itself in many of the histories, traditions, and folktales of the area, taking the seeker of the strange and unusual to remote and out-of-the-way places.

Such a place might be Beetor Cross, where a spectral highwayman with skeletal features and hollow eyes, wrapped in a dark cloak, awaits any traveler who passes that way once darkness has fallen. It could be Bradford Pool, where a soft and alluring voice calls to passers by, drawing them into the water and to their deaths. Or it could be Cadover Bridge, where the sounds of a phantom battle echo continually during both day and night. One of the most common specters to prowl the lonely moor is that of a great black hound or Devil Dog. Indeed, such ghostly creatures are a feature of English folklore and are to be found in many places from the barghast of Yorkshire through Black Shuck of Norfolk and Essex to the Doom Dogs of Cornwall. There is also the Church Grim, the hideous hound-like guardian of churches and graveyards that may be familiar because it serves as the template for the Grim who appears in *Harry Potter and the Prisoner of Azkaban*. Some of these canines are said to be the physical embodiment of Satan.

In Devon, these Devil Dogs are known as "Yeth Hounds" or "Yell Hounds" and are said to be the souls of children who have died unbaptised. Some are said to have no head, while some have great large skulls with massive jaws, and many have red and burning eyes, or drip fire from their mouths. References to the Yeth Hound appear in the Denham Tracts—a collection of pamphlets and writings collected by Michael Denham, a local tradesman between 1846 and 1859, which give an insight into the folklore of the county.

Perhaps the most famous of all the Devil Dogs appears in a Gothic work of detective fiction. In August 1901, Sir Arthur Conan Doyle began the latest serialized adventure of his celebrated consulting detective Sherlock Holmes in *The Strand Magazine*. The series, which would run until April 1902, was set against the wild landscape of Dartmoor and concerned the investigation of a curse that haunted an ancient family there. The curse centered on a great black hound, which was supposed to hunt and kill members of this family because of an ancient wrong that had been done. The series was so popular that late in 1902, the serialized sections were brought together in a book, which became an immediate best-seller. The adventure was *The Hound of the Baskervilles*. The book has never been out of print and the tale has formed the basis of many films and television adaptations. It is probably the best-known of all Conan Doyle's stories, and is by far the most popular of all the Sherlock Holmes adventures.

The origin of the Baskerville curse originated with Sir Hugo Baskerville—a wild and dissolute man in an earlier time. He held fearsome and blasphemous revelries at Baskerville Hall, and it was during one of these that his wife, a young village maid, managed to escape from the Hall and run out onto the moors. Finding her gone, Sir Hugo set out after her and caught up with her on the moors (in the 1959 film of the book this was in a ruined abbey). Before he could either kill or ravish her, he was attacked and killed by a great hound which appeared out of the mist and was reputedly the spirit of the moorlands. This monstrous animal was supposed to haunt the Baskerville family, and threatened and killed several of its members throughout the years. Sir Henry Baskerville, the new heir to the Hall, was in danger from this ancient legend and Holmes was called in to protect him. Through his detecting skills, the great sleuth determined that a member of a distant branch of the Baskerville family was using the ghostly legend to his own ends and was trying to grasp the Baskerville inheritance by murdering Sir Henry. The spectral hound was exposed as a fraud.

That is the story that flowed from Conan Doyle's pen, but was it based, at least in part, on truth? Was, for example, the legend of Sir Hugo Baskerville based on a real person, and did the story color the author's work? This is where Squire Richard Cabell, whose tomb is to be found in the village of Buckfastleigh, comes in.

If Sir Hugo Baskerville was a dissolute and monstrous man, then Richard Cabell seems to have been even worse. He was the local squire and member of parliament in Buckfastleigh (which lies near the famous Buckfast Abbey, famous for its tonic wine) during the 1600s, and was widely regarded during his lifetime as "the most evil man on Dartmoor"—a reputation which he enjoyed immensely. He had married Elizabeth Fowell, daughter of Sir Edward Fowell, president of the Committee for Sequestration (the body empowered to impose fines issued by the monarch or parliament) who brought with her a fairly large fortune, setting Cabell up as a country gentleman. However, he was not a popular man. Rumours circulated that he had murdered his wife and also several village girls, whom he had taken as servants and sexually abused. The tale concerning the murder of his wife almost parallels the Conan Doyle story precisely. Sick of his excesses, the lady fled from Brook Manor (which Cabell had built for himself in 1656) and out onto Dartmoor, accompanied only by her favorite hound. Cabell pursued her, caught her, and killed her on a lonely stretch of moorland. However, as he delivered the final blow, the hound leapt upon him and tore his throat out. This tale is, of course, pure fiction, as Cabell's wife outlived him by some 14 years. The servant girls may be a slightly different matter. Nevertheless, he was a reputed drunkard and gambler, and it was said that he practiced black magic on the grounds of Brook Manor and that he'd sold his soul to the Devil. In the early days of the English Civil War, Cabell openly declared his unswerving loyalty to the King,

Charles I. He declared that he would "defend the Monarch with his last drop of blood." However, as the war progressed and the king looked as if he might lose, Cabell began to have second thoughts. In 1647, he was fined by parliament for his Royalist sympathies, but he quickly recanted, denounced the king, was pardoned, and had his lands and fine returned to him. Perhaps it was this which turned his tenants and a number of local landowners against him and contributed to the tales that were told about him—Buckfastleigh was an area in which Charles was held in extremely high regard.

On July 5th, 1677, Richard Cabell finally died and was laid to rest in Holy Trinity Church, perched on a rocky outcrop looking toward Buckfast Abbey. Today, the church is no more than a shell, but as the visitor walks toward it, he or she is confronted by a massive fortress-like tomb known as "the Sepulchre." This is Cabell's tomb, and it is said that it was built to "keep him in." Indeed, "the Sepulchre" looks more like a prison than anything else, and peering through the iron bars that mark its front, one is struck with a chill, as if *something* inside was reaching out in order to make its presence known. During his lifetime, Cabell was a keen huntsman and kept a pack of exceptionally ferocious dogs, which were "the terror of the countryside" (some traditions, however, ascribe the ownership to his grandson Thomas who owned the first pack of hounds in Dorset). These hellhounds are now supposed to circle the old churchyard on certain nights of the year, led by Cabell himself, sometimes appearing as a tall dark-cloaked man, and sometimes as a great dog. In order to keep the soul of the evil squire from rising, a great stone was placed over his tomb in the family vault, but this doesn't appear to have worked very well. It was once a great game among children in the area to go up to the tomb, run around it counterclockwise seven times, and push their fingers through the iron grille and into the darkness beyond. The story was that if they were bad, Cabell would give them a bite. However, a number of locals claim to have seen a strange red light emanating from behind the bars to signal that the evil squire was stirring.

Beneath the tomb and the church lies a system of caves that extends for about 3.5 kilometers. In one of the larger caverns, known as "Reed's Cave" stands a curious figure known as "the Little Man." Created by the fusion of a stalactite and a stalagmite, it resembles a small human figure in 17th-century clothes. Eerily, it is said to stand exactly beneath the tomb of Richard Cabell and local imagination has often connected the two. Folklore states that this curious formation—although natural—may contain the very essence of the evil squire and allows his influence to permeate through the graveyard attached to the now-abandoned church and beyond. It is also said that ghastly creatures—specters, demons, and hobgoblins—gather there at night in order to receive instruction from their master who lies above them in his grave.

The graveyard has a sinister reputation. During the late 18th and early 19th centuries, it was allegedly the haunt of bodysnatchers (although this has never been verified and any details concerning the activity would appear to be sketchy) who apparently dug up freshly buried bodies at the behest of local doctors. The remoteness of the site and an enclosed, shadowy lane that led down to the church would have provided cover for their activities. Even today, a number of local residents have seen shadowy figures moving through the graveyard at night—perhaps the ghosts of "Resurrection Men." "It's difficult to make out who they are," said one present-day resident who asked not to be named. "They may be ghosts, although there was some talk that witches used to use this place for their meetings."

The church has been burned twice. In the first incident, arsonists broke into the building in May 1849 and set fire to the vestry, much of which was destroyed, together with part of the roof, some of the north aisle, and the communion table. In 1992, another fire was started under the altar. When summoned, the local fire brigade had trouble pumping water (the nearest hydrant was over a quarter of a mile away—added to the difficulty that the water had to be pumped uphill) and the blaze managed to take hold of the building. The fire was blamed on Satanists who it was alleged were using the church and Cabell's tomb for their rituals, although this was never proven. Recently, most of the church and the tomb have been closed off with a stout fence.

So is Richard Cabell truly the inspiration for Sir Hugo Baskerville in Conan Doyle's novel, and does his restless spirit still prowl the countryside in the guise of a monstrous hound? In 1901, the author visited Cromer Hall in Norfolk with his old friend Bertram Fletcher-Robinson who lived at Ipplepen in Devon. The Hall was then owned (and still is) by the Cabel-Manners family and the two men were invited to dinner by Benjamin Bond Cabell—a direct descendant of the dark squire. During dinner, they discussed the squire and also the local legends of Black Shuck, the Devil Dog of the area. The germ of an idea may have been placed in Conan Doyle's mind. Later that year, Fletcher-Robinson took his friend on a tour of Dartmoor where they visited Brook Hall (built by Cabell), Grimspound, and the Fox Tor Mires (later to become Great Grimpen Mire in the novel). Their coachman on the tour was Fletcher-Robinson's young servant, Harry Baskerville; impressed with the grand-sounding name, Conan Doyle would later use it for the name of his family and the coachman as a template for Sir Henry. Many have argued that Cabell's home at Brook Manor served as the model for Baskerville Hall, but the description seems to owe more to that of Cromer Hall in Norfolk where the author and his friend dined with the dark squire's descendant. There is no doubt that the story of Richard Cabell served as a basis for the novel.

But does his spirit still wander the moors? Standing by his tomb in the grounds of Holy Trinity churchyard as the light fades, it is easy to think so. Especially when, away in the distance, you hear the cry of some far-away hound!

Capuchin Cemetery

Palermo, Sicily

"Oh ye Dead! Oh ye Dead!
Whom we know by the light you give,
From your cold gleaming eyes,
though you move like men who live."
—Thomas Moore, *Irish Melodies Vol. 8*

What does death *really* mean? The end of an involvement in all worldly things? To be laid away in the ground and more or less forgotten about, marked only by a stone? Or to preside over a court of decaying and rotting cadavers in a network of underground chambers and tombs, dressed in your most splendid clothes? How creepy is *that?*

The ancients often had very different ideas about death than we do today. For them, death was probably not the end and the deceased were often well-aware of what was happening in the world of the living. And from time to time, they could and would intervene (sometimes in corporeal form) in everyday affairs—to warn, advise, punish, or reward. They could also serve as protectors to a clan or family. Evidence has shown us in places such as Ireland, Norway, and Peru that early civilizations, which, in some cases followed a tradition of ancestor worship, created monuments, cairns, and even small houses for the rotting cadavers of the deceased. These monuments were placed close to the main settlements, so the dead could be consulted on various matters. Although deceased, their strength, courage, and wisdom were still highly valued amongst their descendants. The dead hadn't really gone away and their physical presence served as a tangible connection with the world of the living. Death was no hindrance to them; it was probably just the route to another plane of existence.

Something of the same cultural viewpoint lies behind the creation of crypts and catacombs in which the dead are sometimes placed. Within the confines of such places, the dead stand or sit, dressed in their full clothes or robes, just as they did when alive. Here, the distinction between life and death is in no way stark. And such places are often the last resting place of the important and the wealthy—for example, the Roman Christian catacombs beneath several of the major ancient Roman streets, contain the remnants of the early martyrs and fathers of the Church.

Perhaps rivaling the Roman chambers are those of the Capuchin monastery in Palermo, Sicily. The cemetery and catacombs are part of a larger monastic complex that was built in Palermo (originally a Phoenician town) around 1533. The main cemetery was used for the burial of the town's important Catholic families, and, with the monks also being buried there, it quickly became overcrowded. The monastic center in Palermo also attracted large numbers of ex-Franciscan monks (the Capuchins returned to the basic ideals of St. Francis) from all over Southern Italy, many of whom died within the monastery and were buried there, taking up more and more space; by the end of the 16th century, the cemetery was full. Bizarrely, when Brother Silvestro of Gobbio died at Palermo in 1599, his body was lowered into a disused well on the monastic property. When his body was inspected within a year, it was mummified—perhaps something to do with the tufaceous soil in the area, which produced a warm, dry atmosphere within the well cavity. A similar phenomenon took place in an area below St. Michan's Church near Smithfield in Dublin where three mummified cadavers have been the subject of much curiosity for many years. It takes between eight to nine months for the flesh of the body to completely dry out and give a brownish, slightly wizened appearance. In some cases, it dries out so completely that dried bone is exposed. The mummification, however, was taken as a sign of supreme holiness, and soon, several other monks wished to be mummified. The catacombs were dug out in the monastery complex, and while this was going on, some bodies were laid out in specially prepared underground "cells" known as "strainers" so that they could be preserved.

Originally, the catacombs were intended only for the Capuchin monks—a sign of their holiness and of the sanctity of their lives. Bodies were laid out on ceramic cylinders to be dried, and sometimes vinegar and herbs were applied to the skin in order to make it dry quicker. Those who were considered especially holy were embalmed and sometimes enclosed within upright glass cases where they could look out upon the palace of the dead around them. The monks were often preserved in their robes complete with crucifixes, holy medallions, and various ropes and cords, which they had worn as penances. However, the notion of sanctity coupled with the idea of being buried in the catacombs greatly appealed to the wealthy of Palermo and beyond. Mummification and burial in the crypts became fashionable, and for a fee, the rich were also laid to rest in the crypts. Some stood, some sat, some were laid out in open, glass-covered coffins. All were set out in life-like poses and dressed in a grandiose style. Some were set together in groups as though chatting or gossiping. The catacombs had various sections—one for the monks, one for priests of the Church, one for professionals, one for children, and one for women (virgins had a special section all to themselves and were identified by metal headbands). The children's section is particularly poignant, because even babies are interred there, dressed in their christening shawls. Young girls were laid to rest in their confirmation dresses, and the boys were dressed in small suits.

The catacombs are actually part of the overall cemetery and entrance to them is gained through the continuing wall, which actually forms part of the graveyard enclosure with a throughway that leads to the church. The crypt is large, more than 20 feet high, with a vaulted ceiling with individual tombs and "funeral houses" leading off. As mummification became more and more popular, the catacombs filled rapidly. It is thought that, today, they house the remains of more than 1,000 citizens, not including the monks who are interred there. Their families could come to the tombs on a regular basis to pray for the repose of their souls and sometimes to leave small offerings to an especially holy relative. They could even sometimes hold the hands of the dead during prayer or kiss their dead cheeks in order to give them a measure of comfort. Once again, there was little barrier between the living and the dead.

Mummification was outlawed in Italy in 1881 and the practice of having the remains of a holy person or loved one placed in the catacombs stopped. However, there was one last exception that was made: the case of 2-year-old Rosalia Lombardo, the daughter of a military leader in the Italian Army, who died in December 1920 from advanced pneumonia. Her grieving father, General Lombardo, a wealthy and powerful man, hired Dr. Alfredo Salafia, a noted Italian embalmer, to preserve her body. The specially embalmed body was then laid in a glass topped coffin on a marble plinth in a small chapel just off the main concourse (although it was moved in the 1990s). Some investigations by the magazine *National Geographic* into the Capuchin tombs in the late 1990s revealed a slight decomposition, so the coffin was moved to an even drier spot. Nevertheless, her body was in an almost perfect state and according to one account; she looked like she was "merely sleeping." Others state that she was "like a little doll." The last priest to be buried there was Brother Ricardo, a monk from the Palermo abbey, in 1871.

A number of famous people have been interred in these tombs, including several prominent figures in the Italian army as well as the French General Enea DiGuiliano who died in 1848 and is preserved in full Bourbon French military uniform. Others include senior clergymen (often dressed in their full pontificals of office), doctors, sculptors, architects, and writers. Allegedly, the Spanish painter Valazquez is also interred there, but the evidence is uncertain and he may have been buried in his native Spain. Nevertheless, the catacombs include many of the celebrated citizens of both Italy and Sicily, all brought together in a society of the dead.

It is only to be expected that with so many dead around, in various poses and in their everyday clothes and robes—the place is often described as a "realm of the living dead"—that the Cappucini Cemetery has acquired a strong reputation for being haunted. Although it is now a rather macabre tourist attraction, the idea that the spirits of the dead are close by hasn't gone away. Many tourists, walking through the labyrinthine thoroughfares of this underground city of the dead, have seen, heard, and felt things that they cannot explain. Many visitors claim that they have heard voices both speaking and calling to them from the surrounding tombs. There have been sighs and whispers close by and some tourists have felt cold breath on their cheek as they pass by a certain glass-enclosed cadaver or a group of skeletal gossips in a gloomy alcove. The very attitudes of the cadavers and skeletons only serve to create such an impression, huddled together as though watching people pass them by with a sinister stare.

The dry underground crypts are also full of shadows, several of which tourists have claimed (on their blogs and Websites) to have seen move of their own volition. Of course, the light is poor within the catacombs (this is all part of the macabre atmosphere that tour organizers often encourage) and it is often uncertain, creating the impression of movement amongst the ranks of cadavers along the walls, crypts, and alcoves. There are also drafts coming and going along the corridors, which can often stir the rotting fabric of the clothing and once again give the illusion of movement to those passing by. That, of course, is the easy explanation. Perhaps the mummified bodies *do* move, just beyond the corner of one's eye. Who is to say that in such a place something *more* than the purely physical remnant of the dead may not linger on?

Other tourists in the catacombs claim to have felt a cold and ghostly touch as they walked through them. According to a number of accounts, some visitors have felt extremely cold fingers touch the skin of their hands or bare arms, or felt someone tug lightly at their sleeves. When they turned around, there was nobody there, but many say that they have felt a distinct chill as if a presence of some sort was not all that far away. This could be evidence that the spirits of the dead do not venture too far from their corporeal bodies in such dank places.

Others still state that they have gotten lost in the endless galleries of the dead. With corridors doubling back on each other and with passageways leading off the main thoroughfare to tombs and crypts, it may be quite easy to become confused and take a wrong turn. However, some claim that they have been deliberately misled by voices and noises, which have led them to believe that they were closer to the main centers of the tombs than they thought, only to be led further into the underground world. It is not an experience that many would care to share—wandering helplessly among those skeletal ranks before we find our way back to the places of the living.

A city of the dead, set below the streets of a modern-living city, where the preserved and skeleton bodies of our ancestors are lost in eternal contemplation—what could be creepier?

Chase Mausoleum

Christ Church, Barbados

"They's hant then they's ghost. Hant is a plat-eye. And a plat-eye some those old timey people what been dead a long time. Ghost is just uh evil spirit."
—Thelma Knox, interviewed by Genevieve Wilcox Chandler in *Coming Through* (Federal Writers' Project)

There is something that is both mysterious and creepy about the Caribbean, especially when dusk settles across the islands. These are the lands of voodoo, obeah, and Mami Wata—slave religions whose origins are almost as old as time itself, but which can still reach out into the modern world. And not only into our own world, but into the world of spirits as well, for such beliefs draw upon the imminence of unseen things that lurk somewhere close by and observe our every move. As the light fails, isolated locations and remote cemeteries in places such as Trinidad, Jamaica, and Barbados take on an eerie, almost sinister aspect, which can unsettle those passing through. It is little wonder that tales of zombies, haunts, and duppies (island ghosts) abound in certain areas. One such place is the churchyard in Oistins, Christ Church Parish, Barbados.

Even in daylight, parts of the cemetery appear sinister. Queer blue shadows seem to come and go of their own volition under the Caribbean sun and there are many stories of unquiet spirits that come and go among the funeral markers. This is an old cemetery that harbors a particularly terrifying legend.

At the entrance to the cemetery and swathed in the gloom of the silent burying ground stands a rather impressive monument. The ornamented entrance to a burial vault measuring 12 feet by 6 feet, it is sunk halfway into the ground, leading to an underground vault. It is built of large cemented blocks of coral. It is known throughout the Caribbean Islands as the Chase Mausoleum, and it has a particularly curious history.

There are many stories about the origins of the mausoleum, all of them confusing and contradictory. However, one story does seem to have a consistency about it. The Chase Mausoleum was built around 1724 for a prominent planter named James Elliot, who requested that the actual burial vault be underground. Despite his requests and specifications about the tomb, however, Elliot wasn't buried there (although his wife Elizabeth, who died on May 14th, 1792, appears to have been) and the vault remained closed for a time. On July 13th, 1807, it was opened again to admit the coffin of Mrs. Thomasina Goddard, and it was found to be completely empty. What happened to the body of Elizabeth Elliot and her coffin (if it had ever been there)? Mrs. Goddard was a member of the Walrond family who had purchased the vault from the Elliots, but had never needed to open it until then. A heavy marble slab lay against the door, and it had not been moved since the last interment, and there was no evidence of any disturbance. The disappearance remained a mystery, but there were some who said that Elizabeth Elliot had never been buried there at all.

Sometime in early 1808, the tomb was acquired by the Chase family, a wealthy and important clan in Barbados, who gave the mausoleum its name. The family patriarch at the time, Colonel Thomas Chase, was the most hated man on the island. He had a vicious temper and mistreated many of the slaves who worked for him. In fact, he was so cruel that they threatened to revolt on several occasions. On February 22nd, 1808, the Colonel's 2-year-old daughter Mary Ann Maria Chase suddenly and inexplicably died and was laid to rest in the tomb. It is said that the Colonel was beside himself with grief. When the tomb was opened, Mrs. Goddard's body was found undisturbed and still in its coffin, and the tomb was sealed again. On July 6th, 1812, the vault was opened again to lay to rest the body of the Colonel's other daughter, Dorcas, who had also died under mysterious circumstances. It was said that Mary was abused by her father. Dorcas had been unable to live with the horror of it all and had starved herself to death and was laid to rest in the mausoleum. Once again, when the tomb was opened, the bodies there were found to be undisturbed. It was when the vault was opened again one month later to receive the coffin of Thomas Chase (who had reputedly died by his own hand) that another mystery was discovered. Something terrible had happened. Mary's tiny casket had been thrown from one side of the vault to the other and now lay against the far wall from where it was originally placed. The coffin had been lined with lead and was quite heavy. At first, this was assumed to be the work of vandals or thieves, but none of the bodies had been buried with any valuables or with anything worth stealing, and the coffins had not been tampered with. Some of the slaves began to talk openly about spirits and witchcraft. The authorities searched around for an explanation but could find none—the vault was both airtight and watertight, and there was nothing that could have disturbed its occupants.

The vault was opened again on September 25th, 1816 to allow the interment of yet another infant—11-year-old Samuel Brewster Ames; a young Chase relative. Before the funeral took place, however, the tomb was inspected as a precaution. What was found inside was a vision of horror. All the coffins, with the exception of Thomasina Goddard's, had been disturbed. Thomas Chase's coffin had been lined with lead and was so heavy it required several men to lift it. According to some accounts, it had smashed into Mrs. Goddard's casket which had broken open, leaving the lady's skeleton poking out in an obscene and horrifying fashion. The vault was tidied up again, with the coffins moved back to their original positions, and the tomb was resealed with the marble slab on top. On September 27th, it was reopened for the body of another relative—and the coffins were found once again to be in severe disarray. No explanation could be given and locals were starting to become seriously worried.

On July 17th, 1819, it was opened yet again to admit the coffin of Mrs. Thomasina Clark (daughter of Thomasina Goddard) and the coffins were again hurled around the narrow vault by an unknown force. By this time, the stories concerning the site had reached epic proportions. Voices and lights were heard and seen, and there was much talk of duppies and voodoo. There was also a rumor that there was a secret entrance to the mausoleum and that the some of the contents of the coffins were being used in dark practices. Fearful of some sort of local uprising inspired by such tales, the authorities stepped in.

One of those who supposedly attended Thomasina Clark's funeral was Stapleton Cotton, 1st Viscount Combermere and British Governor of Barbados. He apparently witnessed the disarray and ordered an immediate and official enquiry. The Chase Mausoleum was carefully and thoroughly inspected. No trace of a secret entrance to the tomb was found, and, although fine sand was scattered on the floor to detect any footprints, none appeared; though one grisly incident was reported during the course of these inspections. As one of the men inspected the walls, the skeletal hand of Mrs. Thomasina Goddard fell out through a hole in the side of her coffin and touched him on the shoulder!

The inspection concluded, and, after replacing the coffins, the governor and his men withdrew, placing the official seal of the colony on the marble slab. On April 20th, 1820, some eight months after the burial of Thomasina Clark, the tomb was reopened again. The official seal was still intact as were a number of secret traps, which had been set up to detect interlopers. But the coffins, with the exception of Mrs. Goddard's, were found to be in disarray. The vault was resealed—although it is unclear as to whether or not the coffins were removed to some other location—and is currently empty. Stories of "hants" and "duppies" still proliferate in the area, and even now, many local people will not approach it after dark.

So is there some evil force surrounding the Chase Mausoleum that somehow affects the coffins of those who are laid within it? Are these events accurate, and are there other instances of such apparent supernatural activity? In some ways, the Chase story parallels another tale concerning the Williams family vault, also on the island of Barbados. General William Asgyll Williams was a Puritan General during the English Civil War who had swapped sides and joined the Royalist cause. At the Restoration of Charles II in 1660, he was accused and found guilty of a number of alleged crimes and was transported to the island of Barbados where his family managed to acquire a tract of land in Welchman's Hall Gully. The family was staunchly Protestant, but one of the General's sons angered his family by marrying a Catholic and having several of his offspring raised in the Catholic faith. When the General's daughter-in-law died at the beginning of the 1700s, she was laid to rest in the family vault. Some years after, when the vault was opened again, it was found that a number of the coffins had moved, apparently of their own volition. The supposition was that the Protestant dead had taken exception to the Catholic interment and had moved their coffins away from hers. This story was well-known across Barbados and may have influenced the tale of the Chase Vault.

The story of the moving dead was first recorded by a clergyman—the Reverend Thomas H. Orderson—who was a minister in Christ Church Parish at the time the events occurred. Orderson recorded them as part of a personal investigation into curious incidents and witchcraft in Barbados. Using Orderson's account Sir J.E. Alexander mentioned the incident in his book *Transatlantic Sketches*, which was published in 1833—13 years after Combermere opened the tomb. He accounts in lurid detail how the decaying arm of Dorcas Chase was hanging over the edge of her coffin and how the others had been upended and were threatening to break open. The account was reprinted in 1903 by the Scottish folklorist Andrew Lang again using Orderson's records. Curiously, in investigating the incident, Lang found no account of the events in any of the local Barbados newspapers. There is, however, another diary account of Nathan Lucas, who witnessed at least some of the events, but there is really no other reference to it anywhere.

This has led a number of people to speculate that the described events never happened at all. Orderson's account is allegedly loaded with secret Masonic symbolism and some writers—for example, Joe Nickell—have argued that the account is an allegorical one. It is argued that this is a heavily coded set of Masonic instructions concerning some sort of hidden "treasure," which is of interest to the Order. The Chase Vault is then some sort of Masonic "gateway" to the hiding place of something important, although nobody can say what it is. Others have claimed that the story is just an amalgamation of old "hant tales" from other parts of the island and is not really a true account at all.

But if the events *did* occur, what caused them? A suggestion that the Vault was flooded is one of the explanations often given. But if this were so, why were *all* the coffins (including that of Mrs. Goddard) moved about? Maybe it was the result of a minor earthquake, but none was recorded. Some have suggested that mysterious natural forces or energies may converge at the Vault and may dislodge the coffins there, but there seems to be little evidence for this. Maybe it was, as some old legends say, the result of supernatural activity—the workings of duppies and ghosts. The marble Chase Mausoleum, set deep in the Caribbean shadows, keeps the secret of its "creeping coffins" even today.

Csejthe Castle

Csejthe, Hungary

"Take some salt, no more than a handful, and mix it with human urine. Place it in a muslin bag and wear it around your neck or place it upon your chest when you sleep."
—A Romanian protective charm against vampires

During the reign of King Mathias II of Hungary (1608–1619) and for a number of years after, the name "Csejthe" was forbidden to be spoken by any Hungarian on pain of death. Today, the once-proud fortress that bears this name is little more than a ruin, but its dark associations linger on in the human mind. Csejthe was a prison, but is more accurately described as a tomb for a murderess whose crimes were so abhorrent and macabre that they could not be spoken about by decent people. And so the name of the prisoner and of her prison were excised from human speech in many parts of Eastern Europe. Nowadays, we have no difficulty in naming the Countess Elizabeth Bathory, referred to by some as the "Countess Dracula."

In many ways, the story of the Countess Elizabeth reflects the troubled history of the area into which she was born during the mid-to-late 1500s, as the forces of Christendom made war against the advancing forces of Islam all through the Eastern regions of Europe. It was a dark and bloody time during which all sorts of ghastly atrocities took place and the Bathory family were often crucial to some of these. They were an old and noble line—one of the oldest in the principality of Transylvania, in fact. They claimed descendancy from a legendary hero, Val Bathory who had reputedly slain a ferocious dragon with a mace in what is now Eastern Romania. It is believed that this legend was the basis for the story of Iorgi, the knight who also slew a dragon and later transformed it into St. George, the patron saint of England. They were also related to many of the clans around them by marriage (some of which were undoubtedly incestuous) and in doing so, acquired large tracts of land. Elizabeth's mother Anna Bathory was the sister of King Stephen of Poland and her father Iorgi (George—her mother's third husband) was ruler of several principalities. But the lineage was plagued with stories of incest and inbreeding, which had led to madness and monstrous births hidden away in remote castles in times past.

Elizabeth was born into this illustrious but greatly troubled family in 1560. Her mother was a devout Calvinist with very strict views and an exceptionally strong character, and her father George was a hard-working man and relatively able administrator within the Hapsburg Empire. She had one elder brother named Stephen (a popular name amongst the Bathorys) and two younger sisters—Sofia and Klara, who have disappeared into history without a trace.

Her family was anxious to make a good marriage for her and also strengthen their position within the region, so at the age of 11, Elizabeth was promised in wedlock to the 15-year-old Count Fenricz (Francis) Nadasdy, fabulously wealthy and reckoned to be one of the most eligible bachelors in Hungary at the time. It was a political marriage designed to move the family closer to the Hungarian throne, but it was advantageous for Fenricz to be associated with such an old and noble lineage. He promptly changed his name to Bathory to cement the association. However, the Bathory name carried its own notoriety as well as prestige.

Fenricz and Elizabeth waited four years before marrying on May 8th, 1575. While her new husband was away fighting the Moslem Turks, Elizabeth was given into the care of her mother-in-law, the formidable Lady Ursula Kasizsai (the Lady Nadasdy). While she was there, plagues and epidemics raged throughout Eastern Europe. Tides of disease and illness combined with human misery lapped at the walls of the Nadasdy Castle at Savarin, keeping everyone confined within its walls. Elizabeth found herself under the control of her dominant mother-in-law (who was widely rumored to have lesbian tendencies). During this time, according to legend, Elizabeth was visited by a mysterious "black stranger" with whom she had a relationship. This was widely reputed to have been a forest demon, conjured up by some of the servants or by her mother-in-law (who was also supposedly a witch). Perhaps, however, she might have had an affair with one of the servants and this may have given her a reputation for promiscuity.

Shortly after her mother-in-law died, Elizabeth joined her husband at the remote Csejthe Castle. Fenricz had taken the lead in halting the Turkish advance and was making something of a name for himself in Christian circles. He was now known as the "Black Hero of Hungary" and Csejthe was being regarded as a bulwark against the oncoming Islamic tide. He was frequently away, leading expeditionary forces against the Muslim armies and leaving his wife alone in the dark and gloomy frontier fortress.

It was now that Elizabeth fell under various malign influences. The servants at Csejthe were mainly local people, steeped in the lore and superstition of the region. This was a remote area, filled with old traditions stretching back centuries and the people reflected this. One servant in particular, an old lady named Anna Dervulia was thought to be a sorceress and greatly knowledgeable in witchcraft, and her influence over Elizabeth appeared to grow in the days when her husband was away. Some sources quote this lady as being the Countess's lesbian lover, but this has not been proven.

In 1600, Count Fenricz was killed in battle against the Turks, making his wife the mistress of Csejthe. However, by this time, she was in her 40s and was starting to show signs of aging. One evening a servant hurt the countess while brushing her hair, and the Countess turned on her and struck her on the back of the hand with the hairbrush, drawing blood in the process. Some of the blood fell on the Countess's skin, and sometime later Elizabeth noticed how fresh the area where the blood had touched her now appeared. She recalled a piece of local lore that whoever bathed in the blood of a virgin girl would have their youth and vigor restored. She therefore embarked upon a trail of mayhem and evil—torturing servants, killing them, and bathing in their blood in an attempt to regain her lost youth and looks. In this, she was aided by Anna Dervulia and some of the other servants—a wet nurse named Illona (Helena) Jo, Dorota Semtesz, her manservant Janos Ujvary (known as Flicko), and a washerwoman Katarina Beneczky. Between late 1600 and 1611, these monsters tortured and killed other servants in many excruciating ways, all guided by the Countess. Even when Anna Dervulia suffered a stroke which left her blind, it didn't stop the others in their terrible pursuits. She disappeared, but the others carried on. Anna Dervulia had ensured that all the girls that had been used in the ghastly crimes had been of peasant stock and therefore when complaints and queries were made, they were largely ignored. However, with Anna out of the way (perhaps even dead) Elizabeth became more reckless and started abducting certain daughters of the lower nobility for her supply of virgin blood. She also took a great delight in sado-masochistic torture and whispers of what was going on at Csejthe soon began to circulate in the countryside. Even so, few dared speak out against her. She then turned to a woman named Erzsi Majorova, the widow of a local tenant farmer, to help her in her procurement and disposal of the young girls. Erzsi was less careful than Anna Dervulia had been and insisted that the murdered girls all received a Christian burial, making a connection with a local priest. At first the Church assisted, but with the numbers of servant girls who had "died" in Elizabeth's employ, the priest gradually became suspicious and reported his doubts to the authorities. Still, nothing was done and Elizabeth began to imagine herself above the law.

However, she made an enemy of the Hungarian King Matthias by demanding that he pay the debts that he owed her former husband. When the monarch refused her requests for money, she began selling off some of her late spouse's castles—some of which had been given to Fenricz by the king himself. This once again drew the unwelcome attention of the Hungarian authorities, raising formal questions concerning her activities. Her cousin, Count Thurzo, the Hungarian prime minister, was forced to intervene in order to stop her selling any more Bathory property, particularly to foreigners. In December 1610, Elizabeth and Erzsi grew exceedingly careless and dumped the bodies of four servant girls from the ramparts of Csejthe in full view of some passing peasants. They had been dumping a number of bodies in local rivers for several months, some of which had been partly devoured by wild animals. Now connections were made and the villagers reported what they had seen directly to the King's representative. Perhaps because of her lineage and status within the country, Elizabeth considered herself untouchable, but both the crown and the Church came together to investigate and ordered Count Thurzo to carry out an unexpected raid on Csejthe. On December 29th, 1610, Thurzo's troops entered the castle. What they found was like a scene from a horror movie. Behind the gate was the body of a servant girl with her internal organs removed while some of the rooms more resembled a butcher's shop than living quarters. There were a number of other dead bodies of which Elizabeth and her cohorts had not been able to dispose.

Overcome by the horror and at a loss at what to do because the evidence against her was so overwhelming, Thurzo decided to place her under house arrest and not bring her to trial. All her confederates, however, had to face the full rigor of the law. Dorota Semtesz and Illona Jo both had their fingers pulled out with red hot pincers and were publicly burned alive. Flicko was beheaded (probably because of his youth) before also being burned. Four red gibbets were erected at each corner of the castle and what was left of the malefactors was put on display for the satisfaction of the villagers, until they eventually decomposed. Accounts are sketchy, but some say that Anna Dervulia was amongst the executed.

King Matthias agreed with Thurzo's decision not to bring Elizabeth to trial—she was to remain under house arrest at Csejthe, but with certain conditions. She was to be confined to two or three rooms, which were to be boarded up, and she would not be permitted to see God's blessed sunlight again. Stonemasons were brought in to seal up the doorways and windows, which allowed no daylight to penetrate her quarters—only a small aperture was left so that her jailers could leave food for her. She was condemned to a living tomb. Her name was not to be spoken anywhere in Hungary again, and all references to her were to be excised from all documents. The Hungarian people—and the world in general—were to forget her completely.

But, of course, they didn't, and even during the remainder of her life, she was secretly talked about and her name was whispered in old folktales. Stories about her grew wilder and wilder—that she was immortal; that she had somehow retained her youth; that even in her grim and lightless world, she was still the most beautiful woman in Hungary; and that she had drunk blood and was a vampire. It is this later connotation that has stuck, and she has become known as "the Countess Dracula."

On July 31st, 1614, Elizabeth (reputedly aged about 54) dictated her last will and testament to two priests from the Estergom bishopric. What remained of her family holdings were to be divided among her children, with her son Paul and his descendants receiving the major portion. Shortly afterward, one of the guards decided that he would try to look at her through the aperture through which she was fed—after all, she was once said to be the most beautiful woman in the country. When he looked through, however, he could just about see the body of the Countess lying face down on the floor. The monster that had killed so many servants and had bathed in their blood was dead in her own lightless world.

Records concerning Elizabeth's life and her hideous crimes were sealed for 100 years. The name *Csejthe* became a swear word in Hungarian and the Slovaks who dwelt within the borders of the country often referred to the Countess obliquely as "the Hungarian whore." And yet, the shadow of Elizabeth Bathory continued to hang over the country—and further afield—like a dark and musty cloak. She has appeared in books, stories, and films, most notably *Countess Dracula* (1971) starring Ingrid Pitt, becoming almost as famous in her own way as Dracula himself. Was she a vampire, a monster, or simply insane? That is a question that's never been answered.

Her ghost is still supposed to haunt Csejthe, the place of her tomb-like imprisonment. A number of visitors to the ruin claim to have seen strange shadows drifting through the fallen archways or heard eerie cries echoing from some unknown but far away location—perhaps the Countess's death cries? Her former presence there seems to have left an eerie pall over the place, which lingers down to the present day.

"The stone walk is paved with dark cries."
—Pierre-Jean Jouve

Dragsholm Castle

Dragsholm, Denmark

"...it is as though they haunt for haunting's sake—much
as we relive, brood and smoulder over our pasts."
—Elizabeth Bowen, Preface to *The Second Ghost Book*

If it's ghosts you want then Dragsholm Castle (Dragsholm Slot) in Denmark is said to have more than 100 of them. The fortress is without question, one of Scandinavia's most haunted sites, and reflects its turbulent history and those who inhabited its frowning walls.

Although today the castle is a Baroque building, it stands on the remains of an earlier medieval structure. Indeed, there has been a fortress on the "Drag" (isthmus) of Odsherred since the early 13th century. Prior to the damming of the Lammefjord (a large inlet), the settlement of Odsherred was connected to the rest of Zealand by a dag or draugh—a small strip of land, and the Castle (which lay to the east) was supposed to protect this. It was built around 1215 by Peder Sunesen, titular Bishop of Roskilde, although he never lived to see it fully completed (he died in 1214). His successor, Neils Stigsen, later secularized the diocese and the castle, and while still the property of the Bishops, became home to many nobles and churchmen. In fact, a man who is counted as the last Catholic Bishop of Roskilde, Joachim Rannow (1529–1536), was briefly incarcerated there, before being taken to Copenhagen Castle, where he died in 1544. Although he is count-ed as a Bishop, Rannow was never consecrated, nor did he formally hold the Epis-copal properties, but nonetheless his troubled spirit still haunts Dragsholm and can be seen in full robes wandering in various areas of the Castle in which he was a prisoner. For some reason, his predecessor Lage Ume (Bishop from 1512–1529) also haunts the building and has been seen by a number of people.

It was during the stormy events of 16th-century Denmark that the castle came to ghostly prominence. It became one of the central conflicts during the Grevens Fejde (the Count's War—1534–36), which was an important turning point in Danish history as it ushered in the Protestant Reformation across the country. Following the death of King Frederick I, the nobles of Jutland rose in revolt and deposed his Catholic successor (and co-ruler) Christian II, replacing him with Frederick's own son Christian (Christian III), who was staunchly Prot-estant. However, Christian II had some very powerful support in his home area of Oldenburg where the Protestant Count Crisoffer raised an army in his support, sweeping through Denmark, burning and pillaging. Castles fell before his army, but Dragsholm held out—the only castle in Zealand to do so—and even man-aged to drive the Count's forces back. However, many were killed in defense of the fortress and their ghosts are still attached to the place. Many have heard the sounds of a 500-year-old siege echoing around its walls.

On June 11th, 1535, Count Crisoffer was finally defeated at the Battle of Oksneberg by the armies of Count Johan Rantzan, opening the way for the siege of Copenhagen and the end of the War. The victor, Christian III, ruled as a repres-sive and absolutist monarch, and this meant a change in status for Dragsholm.

The castle now became a prison. Christian had been so impressed with its impenetrability that he assumed it would make an excellent place of incarceration—those who had failed to break into it would now fail to break out. Its prisoners however, came from the upper ranks of both the nobility and the clergy and someone could be imprisoned simply for insulting the king. Denmark was still in a very shaky state with Sweden casting greedy eyes in its direction and king Christian was determined to hold onto power and maintain stability of his throne. He trusted no one, not even the nobles from Jutland, who had brought him to the throne. A number of prisoners were thrown into Dragsholm and the cries of the incarcerated are still said to reverberate around the castle walls.

Although it held many prisoners, one of the most famous to be incarcerated in Dragsholm was James Hepburn, 4th Earl of Bothwell and 1st Duke of Orkney (1534–1578), third husband of Mary, Queen of Scots. Following the Battle of Carberry Hill, East Lothian in Scotland (1567) in which Mary's forces were defeated, Hepburn fled to Scandinavia in the faint hope of receiving backing from Frederick III of Denmark and Norway, and raising an army there to put Mary back on the Scottish throne. Unfortunately, his ship was seized by the Norwegian navy and he was taken as a prisoner (he had no proper papers) to the port of Bergen. There he was lodged in the house of a noblewoman named Anna Throndsen with whom he had apparently enjoyed a relationship around 1557 (in Flanders he had persuaded her to sell all her possessions in order to finance his gambling). He is alleged to have asked her for more money. Anna could take no more and raised a complaint against him, mainly for the return of the substantial sum she had given him in Flanders as a dowry and which he had gambled away—a complaint which was back by her kinsman, the powerful Erik Rosenkrantz, a leading political figure in Norway. Although Anna softened toward him (perhaps she still had feelings for him) her kinsmen still pursued the claim, despite his offer to them to take his ship as compensation. Moreover, King Frederick had heard that Hepburn was wanted by the English Crown for the suspected murder of Mary's second husband Henry, Lord Darnley, in 1567 and thought that he might profit from keeping Hepburn as a prisoner. At first, Frederick treated Hepburn well, but later he was sent to Dragsholm Castle where he allegedly went mad due to the conditions in which he was kept. He was supposedly chained to a pillar, which is still sometimes shown to visitors, together with a circular track worn in the floor which is said to have been made by his pacing feet. He allegedly died at Dragsholm, and his supposed mummified body was displayed to tourists at nearby Farevejle Church. The actual identity of the body has, however, never been conclusively proven and some authorities say that he was imprisoned there for no more than five years. This does not prevent Hepburn's insane ghost from haunting the Castle and indeed he is one of its main phantoms, appearing and gibbering to several visitors and rattling his chains at them. Apparently his specter is most terrifying to behold. From time to time, too, the sound of horses hooves can be heard in the cobbled yard, and this is also taken to have some connection to Hepburn and his incarceration at Dragsholm.

Yet another mad ghost who still continually makes its presence felt is that of Ejier Brockenhuus, the so-called "Mad Squire." The Brockenhuus family was a very powerful one in Denmark, but were always suspected of being involved in strange practices. They had been involved with the famous Danish witch Christinze Kruckow (one of very few Danish nobility that was executed for alleged witchcraft) during the reign of King Christian IV, a monarch with a great interest in witchcraft (and in its persecution). Ejier Brockenhuus was a noted profligate, who was almost (it's said) uncontrollable in his excesses. Accused of plotting against the King, he was imprisoned in Dragsholm where, once again, he went completely insane (although there are those who assert that he was insane before he was imprisoned). His mad laughter can frequently be heard echoing through the Castle, sending a chill down the spines of all those who hear it.

On June 1st, 1657, the simmering tensions between Denmark and Sweden finally exploded into open conflict as the Danish King Frederick III formally declared war on King Charles X Gustav of Sweden. Sweden won the conflict with the celebrated and unexpected March Across the Belts in which the Swedish king led his army across the Great and Little Belts from Jutland to Zealand. During this time, an attempt was made to blow up Dragsholm, which was only partially successful, but killed a number of people and left the Castle more or less a ruin. It was given, as part of King Frederick's outstanding debts to a grocer, Heinrich Muller, who really did nothing with it.

In 1694, the ruins were sold to the nobleman Fredrik Christian Aldeler, who finally built the Baroque castle that is standing. The family also made several improvements to the surrounding land, including the draining of the Lammefjord by one of Aldeler's relatives who was an engineer. The Aldelers finally died out in 1932 and Dragsholm Castle passed into the hands of the Central Land Board who sold it to the Bottger family, which only included the main estate and not its subsidiary lands. They have been continuously running it since then and the castle has now been developed into a hotel. The place has been modernized slightly, but certainly retains some of the former architecture and antiquities of its violent past.

Besides the spectres of James Hepburn, Ejier Brockenhuus, and the soldiers who died in Dragsholm's defence, several other phantoms haunt its corridors. One of the most regular is said to be the Grey Lady who is rumoured to be actually the spirit of a minor noblewoman who was employed in the Castle. She was

apparently troubled with a painful toothache and sought help from some of the servants who eventually cured her. Out of gratitude she wanders the Castle corridors determining that all's well. Many have felt her presence there and a few have seen her. She appears to be a relatively harmless ghost.

A much sadder phantom is the so-called White Lady, whose story is a more tragic one that involves a love affair. A high-born young lady fell for one of the more lowly born workers, but because of her high status, they had to keep their affair secret from her father. Nevertheless, her father found out and in a fit of rage forbade the girl to see the boy again. When she ignored the prohibition and the lovers were caught, they were separated. The girl was imprisoned within the walls of Dragsholm Castle until she came to her senses. Instead, she made a bridal gown for herself in defiance of her father's instructions. She also passed notes to her lover from her prison. This infuriated her father, who in a fit of blind and total rage ordered her to be walled up within the prison so that her lover would never see her again.

For a long time, this was thought to be just an old and fanciful story representative of the bloody history of Dragsholm. However, during the early part of the 20th century, some workmen were tearing down part of an old wall in order to make way for a new toilet block within the Castle when, behind some plasterwork, they came upon the skeleton of a woman dressed in what appeared to be the remnants of a white bridal gown. Some say that the skeleton was very small and might be more representative of a child—and that the dress was an ordinary white one—which would tie in with the story of the child who is said to wander through the Castle each night. Whether this is the spirit of the White Lady or some other ghost is unknown. No story concerning the death and walling up of a child is associated with Dragsholm, as far as is known.

While staying in the hotel, several people claim to smell a stench similar to gunpowder in some of the rooms and passageways. Could this be some phantom remnant from the battles that once raged around the Castle, or from the attempt to blow it up during the war? And of course there are the groans, insane laughter, and far-away screams that others suggest they have heard. What is *their* origin? Perhaps the terrors of that ancient place are not completely consigned to the past!

Eilean Mor

The Flannan Isles, Scotland

"Though three men dwell on Flannan Isle,
To keep the lamp alight,
As we steered under the lee we caught,
No glimmer through the night."
—Wilfred Wilson Gibson, *Flannan Isle*

Where does our own reality end and another begin? Are there places in the world where the two overlap and where the inhabitants of our own existence might be swept away into another? Or perhaps where beings from somewhere else can cross into our own sphere of existence? If there are, then these locations may be pretty remote and inaccessible to human travellers, and yet they may exist. If they do, then perhaps Eilean Mor in the isolated Flannan Isles could be one such place.

The Flannans, also known as the Seven Hunters, are a group of small islands lying to the west of the Hebridean island of Lewis. Most of them are small and barren, but the largest of them are Eilean Mor (the Big Island), Eilean Taighe (House Island), Soay (Eastward Isle), and Eilean na Gobha (Island of the Blacksmith). Little more than the large crowns of undersea mountains, they have nevertheless acquired something of a mysterious reputation throughout the years. The most persistent story is that there were originally seven men who were turned into islands by the divine wrath for hunting on the Sabbath day (hence their nickname). The islands take their formal name from St. Flannan of Killaloe, a 7th-century Dalcassian prince from County Clare in Ireland whose followers founded a monastery on remote Eilean Mor (with possibly a hermitage on Eilean Taighe). However, at some time during the 9th century, this holy house was mysteriously abandoned. This may have had something to do with the increase of Vikings on the nearby island of Lewis and repeated raids against lonely monasteries by Norse pirates.

In the centuries that followed, the islands changed hands a number of times as rival clans sought to control the area. No clan, however, attempted to colonize them or build fortifications there, so eerie was their reputation. Indeed, the shepherds of Beasclete in Lewis, who occasionally grazed sheep on Eilean Mor, referred to them as "the other country," an area which was not part of this world. The islands were regarded as a place of fairies and of other supernatural creatures. Strange figures were often seen in the island twilight, and, from time to time, grazing animals disappeared as if they had walked or been lured from one world into another. Fear of the Flannans, and of Eilean Mor in particular, was almost palpable. Indeed arrivals on the island had to perform a certain ritual at the now-ruined monastery, which involved crawling on one's knees in a counter-clockwise direction or else some ghastly harm might befall them. At certain times of the year, the Islandmen tended to stay away from the place altogether.

The modern age caught up with the lonely Flannans around 1895. The seas around the Seven Hunters were incredibly dangerous due to submerged shoals and low-lying reefs as continual hazards. As shipping between the Firth of Clyde and America increased, so did the wrecks, reaching a deadly peak throughout the 1850s. The situation became so bad that in 1895, the Board of Trade considered it imperative to build a lighthouse on Eilean Mor to ensure the safety of vessels in the area. In 1896, it gave permission for a 1,000-candlepower light to be constructed on the island. The lighthouse was designed by David Alan Stevenson and would rise 70 feet high on the top of a steep cliff that fell away into the sea 150 feet below. It was built by George Lawson of Rutterglen at a cost of £6,914.1s.9d, which included the building of two jetties with a further £3,526.16s. for a station house for the wives and families of the keepers back in Beasclete. There was to be no radio link between Lewis and the islands, and once out on the island, the keepers were pretty much on their own.

Construction stayed on pace between 1896 and 1899. There were a few curious incidents, including the deaths of two builders who inexplicably fell off of the cliff. Even so, some of the men working on the lighthouse complained about the feeling of a brooding presence somewhere nearby watching them as they worked. Some claimed to hear strange voices calling to them, but these were shrugged off as the eerie cries of the gulls that wheeled about the high cliffs. Finally, early in December 1899, the first light was turned on.

The light had a distance of 20 miles and flashed every 30 seconds and could be seen as far away as Gallen Head in Lewis. The region was prone to heavy fogs, which might obscure the light, but given the amount of shipping in the area, this was considered to be a risk worth taking. The station was to be manned by four keepers working on a rotation—three stationed on the lighthouse and one relief keeper. Every 20 days, the supply tender *Hesperus* would travel from Lewis out to the Flannans to bring fresh provisions, empty supply containers, and carry the relief keeper who would alternate with one of the others on the island. The island staff would consist of a Principal Keeper with two assistants. Because there was no radio contact, the Northern Lights Board paid a local man, Mr. Roderick MacKenzie to observe the lighthouse daily from Gallen Head and report any problems.

The staffing of the Flannan Isle Lighthouse was given to Robert Muirhead, superintendant of lighthouses for the Northern Lights Board. As Principal Keeper, 43-year-old James Ducat, an affable and experienced married man from Arbroath. With him were two assistants, William Ross and Thomas Marshall. Marshall was 28 and had five years' experience as a keeper at the time, was unmarried, and lived at home with his father and at least one sister. He may have been the main breadwinner in his family; following the events at the end of December 1900, his father John tried unsuccessfully to seek compensation from the NLB. Ducat was not terribly happy with the posting. The Flannans were very remote with no radio contact and he pointed out he had a young family of four children, one of whom (Anna) was only seven years old at the time, and the stress on them would be immense. The Board, however, wanted a reliable and experienced First Keeper, and Ducat had 21 years unblemished service; eventually Muirhead persuaded him to go. Ducat would spend 14 months out on the Flannans during the construction of the lighthouse, familiarizing himself with the islands and the conditions there. Before the lighthouse was opened, Muirhead traveled out there to reassure him, but once more Ducat expressed reservations. The seas around the Flannans were sometimes rough and the islands were cut off for long periods. Once again he raised the absence of a radio. What if there was to be an emergency—who would know? Muirhead strove to reassure him, pointing out that the last major accident concerning a lighthouse had occurred around 1850 when a supply boat on its way to the Little Ross Light off Kirkcudbright had been swamped by a giant rogue wave and an entire relief crew had been lost. Nothing like that would happen on the Flannans. Ducat grudgingly accepted the posting and would continue as Principal Keeper of the Flannan Lighthouse for around a year, his last tour of duty beginning on December 7th, 1900.

During the long, lonely days of 1900 the men worked steadily in the lighthouse. Toward the end of the year, Second Assistant William Ross (who hadn't been in good health for some time) went on extended sick leave and Thomas Marshall suddenly found himself promoted to Acting Second Assistant. His place was filled by a rotation of Occasional Keepers from Lewis. In December 1900, the Occasional Keeper was 40-year-old Donald McArthur from Breasclete. A former soldier and tailor by trade, McArthur was highly respected on Lewis. He had married an Englishwoman who had become the island nurse, and both were very popular. One of their two children—their son Calum (Challum an Nurs)—was a prominent pupil at the local school. A staunch member of the Free Presbyterian Church, McArthur was also involved in building a new Meeting House in Breasclete, acting as project manager. In fact, he'd been overseeing the work the day before he set sail for the Flannans.

It must have been a terribly claustrophobic existence for the three keepers, Ducat, Marshall, and McArthur, confined in a narrow lighthouse on a tiny island in the middle of a raging ocean with only the gulls and the occasional seal for company. The islands were bleak and scoured by fierce winds that roared across their barren landscape, sometimes strong enough to carry a man from his feet, and so the three men stayed close to the lighthouse. Things became worse after the 12th of December when a heavy fog rolled in and the Flannans were cut off from the rest of the world. No ships could reach them and they were on their own. The lighthouse would not be visible from Gallen Head for more than a fortnight and the keepers' sense of isolation grew steadily worse.

Battling through heavy seas around midnight on December 15th, 1900, the steamship *Archtor*, bound from Philadelphia to Leith radioed that "no beacon flashed from the Flannan Lighthouse, northwest of Cape Wrath." Her captain thought this was unusual—although there was a fog, he was passing close enough to the islands to make out the flash every 30 seconds. This was a new light and it should be functioning properly. Docking in Oban, Captain Holman made a further report to the Northern Lights Board, recommending that they investigate the failure of the light. The Board, however, didn't act immediately.

A period of bad weather kept most ships in harbor until after Christmas Day, so on December 26th, the tender *Hesperus,* under the command of Captain James Harvie, set sail from Breasclete bound for Eilean Mor. There had been no contact with the fogbound lighthouse since Holman's report, and a brooding sense of apprehension fell upon the tender as it rounded Gallen Head.

Soon, the frowning cliffs of Eilean Mor, with the lighthouse perched on their top, were in view, and looking through his binoculars, Captain Harvie's face creased in a puzzled frown. Normally the keepers raised a flag to acknowledge the arrival of the tender, but this time the flagpole was empty, and the empty supply boxes had not been left for collection at the little jetty below the lighthouse. Jim Harvie's concern began to turn to alarm. He knew that James Ducat was a meticulous man and would neglect such an important duty if he could help it. Were the keepers ill? He ordered a blast on the ship's foghorn, hoping to rouse them, but there was no response. The *Hesperus* carried a number of signal rockets and Harvie ordered one of them to be fired to alert the lighthouse to the vessel's presence. It exploded high in the winter air; Harvie waited, but there was no response from the lighthouse—no answering signal from the station rocket house or any shout. There was now no option but to launch a longboat and investigate. The relief keeper Joseph Moore climbed into the bow and together with the Second Mate McCormick they headed for the island. A couple of times, Moore, who knew all three men well, shouted that they were coming, but there was still no reply. They rowed grimly onward, unsure of what they might find.

The first thing both men noted as they climbed onto the jetty was the overwhelming silence. Even the wheeling seabirds overhead seemed to make no sound and Eilean Mor was bathed in a primal quiet as if no creature had ever existed there. While he secured the mooring ropes, Moore climbed apprehensively up to the lighthouse above. Reaching the gate that surrounded the keepers' enclosure, he found it firmly shut. But there was something else that may have been partly Moore's own invention—along the side of the path which led up to the gate lay clumps of a curious type of seaweed, the like of which the relief keeper had never seen before. It was an odd color and seemed to shimmer with some sort of natural illumination. The outer door of the lighthouse was locked, but Moore had a key.

To say that the Flannan Light was cramped would be something of an understatement. The door opened directly into a passage leading to a small kitchen where the men made their meals. Moore found that while the outer door had been firmly secured, the inner kitchen door lay wide open. Apart from one or two things, the kitchen was in perfect order—although not lit the fire had been laid, and the crockery had been washed and neatly put away. However, on the table was a partially eaten meal, and a chair had been thrown over and lay with its back on the floor as if whoever had been eating had been suddenly interrupted and risen from the food in great haste. In the kitchen, the relief keeper noted the fading traces of an unusual smell—something he couldn't identify—which had nonetheless dissipated by the time McCormack joined him from securing the longboat. Moore now checked the storehouse, living area, and sleeping quarters. All the beds had been neatly made, just as if the lighthouse was still occupied. He called each man by name, but there was no answer. The main clock on the kitchen wall had stopped—it needed to be wound regularly and had been allowed to run down. No one had tended to it in a while. Climbing into the lamp turret, Moore found that everything was in order. The lamps had been filled with oil and their wicks trimmed, ready for lighting. Later he said that he fully expected Ducat or one of the others to suddenly emerge and get on with their business, and that it was the sheer *ordinariness* of things that unnerved him the most. Leaving the lighthouse, he and McCormack began a brief search of the island searching among nearby crags and going up to the old ruins of the tiny monastery, but they found nothing. Near the walls of the church, however, Moore thought he heard a voice calling, but he only heard it for a moment. It sounded like the voice of James Ducat, whom he knew, but he couldn't be sure. It might have been no more than a seabird. Both he and the Second Mate found nothing though once again both men experienced the feeling that someone or *something* was watching them.

Eventually, Moore returned to the *Hesperus* to inform Harvie of the situation. The captain ordered that he return to Eilean Mor and secure the light, but that a group, led by Harvie, would accompany him and make a thorough search of the island. Maybe bodies might be found. Five men landed on Eilean Mor—Moore, Harvie, the Buoymaster Allan MacDonald, and two seamen, Campbell and Lamont—and began a painstaking search of the place. The lighthouse yielded further mysteries. The oilskins that hung in the store belonging to Ducat and Marshall were gone, but those belonging to Donald McArthur still hung there. Had something happened that had caused two of the keepers to don their outdoor clothes and go outside? And had McArthur followed them hastily, simply wearing only his shirt sleeves?

Down at the second jetty, they found evidence of a ferocious storm that had lashed the Flannans. The jetty had been battered as had the surrounding railings, and the mooring equipment was badly warped. A small store that held winding gear was missing, and a toolbox that had been stored there was found open and with its contents scattered halfway up a cliff. Ropes that had also been stored there were found wrapped around a temporary crane 7 feet above normal sea level. Had the keepers perished in a storm? Harvie wasn't sure. He ordered a general search of the island for some trace of the men whom he now believed to be dead. This didn't take long—Eilean Mor was only 39 acres and was so barren that any trace of a body couldn't remain hidden for long. However, they found nothing and eventually went back to the lighthouse. Perhaps, Harvie reasoned, if he examined the keepers' log, he might get some clue as to what happened to the men. It is here that the mystery deepened.

According to some sources, Harvie (and later Robert Muirhead) scanned the log and found something curious. From December 7th when he had commenced duty, James Ducat had carefully recorded the standard observations of any keeper— the tides, the currents, the fogs, passing ships, the moods of the sea. After December 12th, however, Ducat's neat copperplate writing suddenly gave way to the broader hand of Thomas Marshall as Acting Second Assistant:

December 12th
Gale N. by NW. Sea lashed to a fur. Never seen such a storm. Waves very high. Tearing at the lighthouse. Everything ship-shape. James Ducat irritable.
Storm still raging, wind steady. Stormbound. Cannot go out. Ship passing and sounding foghorn. Could see the cabin lights, Ducat quiet Donald McArthur crying.

December 13th
Storm continued through the night. Wind shifted W by N. Ducat quiet. McArthur praying.

There was no entry for December 14th, but there was an undated entry that seemed to be from the 15th.

Noon. Grey daylight. Me, Ducat, and McArthur praying.
1pm. Storm ended. Sea calm. God is over all

Here, it appears, Marshall's account ended with no real indication as to what had befallen him or his companions. Yet, the entries remain the most contentious part of the story. It seems strange that, unless something serious had befallen the Principal Keeper, the Assistant would have taken over the log in such a fashion. Besides, the entries read more like those in a diary than in a formal log, making personal comments about Marshall's companions rather than recording sea conditions. Why in such an important record would Marshall state that Ducat was "irritable"? It could be read by the Principal Keeper's superiors and count against him. And why should a hardened former soldier like Donald McArthur be "crying"? And why should the Assistant Keeper record an overtly religious comment—"*God is over all*" in a station log, especially when it was known that Marshall was not a particularly religious man? And there is one further point to consider. It was the custom for entries to be chalked up on a board beside the

logbook while they were checked for accuracy—for example, wind strengths—before being formally transferred to the page. Some sources say that there were a number of other entries written there that had never been transcribed and that Harvie and later Muirhead had removed. Some others say that the entries in the log were falsified by Harvie to add an element of mystery to the events. The truth of the matter, however, can't be verified, because the Flannan logbook has since mysteriously disappeared and is no longer available.

Captain Jim Harvie was both puzzled and horrified. He had no idea what had happened to the vanished keepers, but he suspected that all three might be dead. His initial conclusion was that they had been somehow carried away by heavy seas at the lower jetty. Perhaps Donald McArthur had been interrupted in his meal and had rushed to help his colleagues without putting on his oilskins and he too had been swept away. Perhaps the original men working on the jetty might have been hit by a freak wave, but a *second* following so closely and striking in *exactly* the same place and taking a third man stretched coincidence a little. All three men were experienced keepers and well used to the ways of the sea, so why should they have been taken so unawares? And why should an experienced keeper and former soldier like Donald McArthur go out into a raging tempest without any form of protective clothing? These were some of the questions that Harvie's theory did not address.

Leaving Joseph Moore in charge of the Light, accompanied by McDonald and the two seamen, Harvie returned to the *Hesperus* and sailed back to Breasclete where he sent a telegram to Robert Muirhead, informing him of what had happened.

A dreadful accident has happened at Flannans. The three Keepers, Ducat, Marshall, and the Occasional have disappeared from the island. On our arrival this afternoon no sign of life was to be seen on the island.

On December 29th, three days after the *Hesperus* had found the lighthouse deserted, Muirhead arrived to conduct a formal NLB investigation. He allegedly found little else, although the rumor still persists that he and Harvie covered certain things up there. Although Harvie had estimated the disappearance of the keepers as being on the 20th of December (six days before the arrival of the tender), Muirhead revised this back to the 15th. He cited the punctiliousness of the log-keeping and the report by Captain Holman of the *Archtor* that no light had been seen then. Harvie's report stated that *every clock in the lighthouse had stopped at exactly the same time*—this assertion was later denied in the official report that said that they had all run down to different times. The men allegedly worked until around mid-day on the 15th, Muirhead concluded, and then something momentous happened. He did, however, agree with Harvie that the keepers had been carried away by the sea. Ducat and Marshall had gone down to the lower jetty to check on storm damage and had been overwhelmed by a wave. Hearing their cries for help, McArthur (who had been eating a meal) had rushed to save them, but had been swept away by a second wave. However, it was pointed out that with the roar of the wind it would be difficult to hear the cries from the jetty up in the lighthouse, so the account was later changed to an situation in which McArthur had actually *seen* the waves coming in and had run to warn the other two. This ignored the fact that it was impossible to see the second jetty from the back kitchen where presumably McArthur had been eating. The difference between all the accounts became more and more confused. Besides the difference regarding the logbook and the clocks, questions were now asked as to whether there actually had been an overthrown chair and a half-eaten meal or whether there had been something else. It was also suggested that there had also been a message written on the keepers' blackboard that either Harvie or Muirhead wiped off. Gradually, however, Robert Muirhead's account was accepted—it tied everything up very neatly and was acceptable to the NLB. That was his job after all, and he carried it out with great efficiency.

At the beginning of 1901, a temporary crew arrived to take over the Flannan Light. The Acting Principal Keeper was John Milne, Principal Keeper at the Tiumpan Head Light, northeast of Stornoway. With him as First Assistant came Donald Jack, and together with Joseph Moore, they manned the remote lighthouse until Muirhead could make his report. Milne, of course, had another brief—to keep an eye out for bodies washed ashore or for anything that would explain the disappearance of the previous keepers. There were a number of rocky crevices (known as geos) on Eilean Mor, and Muirhead thought that perhaps the bodies of the three men would wind up in one of these coastal drains. Milne, however, found nothing. Later he would confess that he didn't like the posting on the island; there was, he said, a "heavy presence" about the lighthouse. A number of times, as he was working, he turned, fully expecting to see somebody there. Several times he thought that he heard voices when Jack and Moore were not present. At the end of his tour of duty, John Milne was glad to leave Eilean Mor behind.

Muirhead's account was fully accepted by the NLB and the mystery was written off as a dreadful accident. Both Ducat and McArthur's wives were paid compensation (the latter returned to England) and the incident was buried in official files. Decades of keepers came and went to the Flannans without further incident, but no trace of the vanished men was ever found. In 1971, the Flannan Light became fully automated and the need for sending keepers to that lonely outpost ceased. However, the disappearance has not been forgotten, and from time to time, it will resurface in local folklore.

So what actually happened to the three keepers on those lonely islands? If we discount the more out-there theories, such as they were carried away by flying saucers or people under the sea, perhaps Harvie's and Muirhead's accounts are the most plausible. Great waves and water spouts have been known to batter the islands during the winter months, and there are many tales of loss of life caused by them around Lewis and beyond. Island people sometimes speak of the *muir cul*, which is said to be a great wave that can rip the turf from the tops of cliffs and can carry away men and livestock. Perhaps that is what hit the Flannans on that fateful day. But *muir cul* can also refer to something else—a monstrous, supernatural evil that creeps in from the sea and attacks lone settlements or houses. It is as shapeless as a sea mist (though it can sometimes take a vague, gigantic human form), but it is always deadly. Could one of the keepers have gone mad, killing the other two and getting rid of their bodies before disposing of himself? Although this sounds rather implausible, it had been known to happen. Claustrophobic living conditions, coupled with the sheer monotony and loneliness of station life, sometimes preyed on a keeper's mind and drove him over the edge of reason. This *might* have happened on the Flannans. Donald John McLeod, the Harbourmaster on Breasclete and an Occasional Keeper in some of the other lighthouses, recalled how he had experienced a situation in which an Assistant Keeper had suffered a mental breakdown after the Principal Keeper had gone down with an exceptionally severe bout of the flu. The man, he said, had become excessively violent, had threatened to kill him, and had to be locked up until the tender *Polestar* had arrived from Stromness, bringing help. It was a particularly terrifying experience, he remembered. And a number of years before the Flannan incident, two keepers had gone inexplicably mad on the lonely Skellig Light off the coast of Kerry in Ireland. Perhaps something like that had happened on Eilean Mor. Nevertheless, it seemed unlikely that three hardened keepers, well used to the loneliness of the islands, would have simultaneously lost their reason.

Among the islands, however, stranger theories surfaced, and old legends suggesting that the Flannans were part of another realm, largely hidden from human eye, re-emerged. Might the keepers, it was asked, have somehow crossed the boundary between one world and the other and be lost to us forever? Might the fearsome storm have opened up a rift between the existences and they were mysteriously drawn through? Old island folk remembered the near-forgotten tale of John Morisone, a fisherman who had been shipwrecked on Eilean Mor at the end of the 17th century. With nothing with which to make a fire and perishing from the cold, he lay down and prepared to die when suddenly out of the dark night an old man had appeared and had led him up to the ruined chapel where a fire was burning behind the altar. The old man gave him a strange warm soup, and although it was dark, Morisone had the feeling that everything around him was somehow *different*. He fell asleep, and when he woke, he was alone in the chapel. He managed to stay alive until rescue came, although his mysterious benefactor had disappeared. Could this person have come out of an invisible world of which the Flannans were said to be a part? Or perhaps he was one of the unseen race, which supposedly dwelt on these bleak islands. Many island people seem to think so, and this perception was strengthened during the 1960s when a number of ornithologists camped overnight on Eilean Mor to monitor puffin and nesting seabird colonies there. During the night, three of them distinctly heard a man's voice crying for help, though there was nobody else on the island, and the sound seemed to be drawing further and further away. This has been variously put down to the wind, the cry of seabirds, or overactive imaginations, but even today people are not all that sure. Maybe it's one of the keepers, still trapped in another world and trying to find a way back into ours.

Or did the powerful storm, as others suggest, throw up something monstrous from the depths of the ocean that attacked the keepers before returning to its lair? Those who support this theory point to the curious seaweed that Joseph Moore supposedly saw on his way up to the lighthouse, which was reputedly cleared away by Harvie and Muirhead, and was eventually omitted from the formal records in some sort of conspiracy. And why has the Flannan log gone missing? Was there some sort of cover-up? Nobody knows for sure.

And there the matter rests, shrouded even today in mystery and speculation. Throughout the years, the eerie disappearance of the Flannan keepers has been overshadowed by investigations into other sea mysteries such as that of the *Marie Celeste* (a brigantine whose entire crew disappeared in the mid-Atlantic) more than 30 years earlier, but that doesn't take away from the sense of menace that the story generates. It has, however, captured the human imagination with a number of articles, plays, an opera and even a *Dr. Who* adventure written around it, keeping the incident on the very edge of our memories. In 1912, Wilfred Gibson wrote his famous poem *Flannan Isle*, which introduced the mystery to many young scholars, although now that it has been dropped, the memory of the strange disappearance is starting to fade.

Today as the sea continually beats against the rocky shores of those distant and remote islands beneath the automated lighthouse, we may well ponder the curious fate of Ducat, Marshall, and McArthur. Are they indeed dead or do they still wait somewhere beyond our knowing, hoping someday to return to the world they left in 1900? Whatever the answer, the lonely Flannans have kept their secret well for more than a hundred years.

> "And as we listened in the gloom,
> Of that forsaken living room,
> O chill clutch on our breath,
> We thought how ill chance came to all,
> Who kept the Flannan Light."

Gore Orphanage Road

Cleveland, Ohio

"The road ahead forked, one path descending into a muddy hollow before rising steeply on the other side to vanish into the brambly thicket; the other leading off under a large hanging archway of branches and creeper into the darkness. Around me little sunlight penetrated the dark trees to light me where I stood and no bird sang."
—L.L. Galbraith, *Cousin Silas's House*

What lurks in the dark woodlands? Is there something moving among the shadows under the trees, just where the sunlight is trying to struggle through? Something that doesn't look quite human, but with a large, misshapen head that's far too big for its body? Something that has disappeared back into the undergrowth? If that's the case, we must be on the Gore Orphanage Road on the outskirts of Cleveland, Ohio.

The legend of the Melon Heads is a common one across several American States, most notably Michigan, Connecticut, and Ohio, but there are older references to them from England and Germany as well. In her *Folklore of Herefordshire* (1955), the English folklorist Mary Letherbarrow mentions an extended family of Melon Heads living on the edge of the village of Risbury. She claims that they had "large, rounded heads," which were thought to be the result of inbreeding. Known locally as "Weeble Heads" they were avoided by the general populace and kept mostly to themselves. Although generally reclusive, they were not exceptionally hostile toward their neighbors. Another Melon Head family allegedly living near Konzenburg in Bavaria, Germany, in the mid-1800s, were not so friendly, and several murders were laid at their door, although nothing was ever proven. They were just as reclusive as those in Risbury, but tended to adopt a more aggressive attitude to those who came near them. And from time to time, in local folklore, stories of Melon Heads—whether just bizarre or highly dangerous—have featured. They have been blamed for doing damage to property or for carrying away small children and vulnerable adults for some unspecified purpose and are therefore feared. They are also said to have a deep and abiding hatred for those whom they consider to be "normal" and are intent on doing them harm.

Where did these Melon Heads come from? In folklore, as is seen in the Risbury and Konzenburg accounts, their origins derive from sustained inbreeding (which was—and perhaps still is—probably more common in isolated communities than we suspect) or illicit sex (for example with the mentally deficient or with animals). In America, stories of mutated and disfigured people were to be found in the remote and inaccessible areas of places like the isolated communities in, say, the Rutherford Mountain area in Tennessee during the 1920s and 1930s, or in mountainous areas of West Virginia. Latterly, however, they are said to be the results of genetic experimentation and manipulation. In recent times, several urban myths have risen around certain groups of individuals, such as vanished children who are believed to have been abducted either by individual scientists or by Government agencies for such purposes. And perhaps nowhere in America is such a variation of the legend so common than in heavily wooded parts of Connecticut, Michigan, and Ohio.

The Kirtland suburb of Cincinnati, Ohio, in particular has achieved a notoriety all of its own concerning the Melon Heads. The area borders on local woodland in which groups of strangely headed humanoids—the results of terrible experiments—are still said to dwell. Even before the alleged advent of the Melon

Heads, one particular area of the suburb had a rather strange and macabre history. This was a site known as Swift's Hollow.

The Hollow takes its name from Joseph Swift, a property developer and land-owner, who moved there from Massachusetts in the mid 1820s, with his wife Eliza, who built a rather large estate house along the Vermillion River, which became known as "Swift's Mansion." According to many authorities, this was the most elaborate and ostentatious dwelling for miles around, and it soon became the talk of the countryside. It was allegedly built in a classic Greek style with won-derful colonnades, the like of which had never been seen before in that region of Ohio. Was it any wonder then that this magnificent building gave the name of its builder to the hollow where it stood? The house was actually called "Rosedale," but its location was always known (and still is) as Swift's Hollow.

Soon after they arrived in the Hollow, bad luck hit the Swift family. In 1831, Swift's 5-year-old daughter Tymphenia died from a mysterious illness, and in 1841, his 24 year-old son Herman also died from a "peculiar wasting." Swift made several bad investments, including several on land initially earmarked for a railroad, that fell through, leaving him almost bankrupt. Swift was forced to sell the grand house in 1865 and move away.

The man he sold it to was Nicholas Wilber, who had a curious reputation. This was an era when spiritualism was taking hold in parts of America and Wilber was greatly interested in the movement. He began to organize "spiritual experi-ments" and séances in the house, much to the alarm of local folk who counted him little more than a black magician. There were various attempts, it was said, to raise both ghosts and demons, all of which haunted the mansion and the sur-rounding Hollow long after the Wilburs were gone.

Similar to the Swift's, bad luck struck the Wilber family shortly after they ar-rived. They lost four of their grandchildren to diphtheria—Jesse (aged 11), May (aged 9), and twins Roy and Ruby (aged 2). All of them died within six days of each other as the disease tore through the mansion between January 13th and January 19th, 1893. Wilber began to suffer from "a strange, wheezy and wasting disease," which may have been related to the diphtheria. His wife died there in 1899 and Nicholas Wilbur died there in February 1901.

After this, the house became abandoned and the notion of a great falling house out in the woods was sufficient to spark ghost stories, especially as attention appeared to be drawn to some "abandoned and overgrown" children's graves out in the undergrowth. Stories of ghosts and walking dead began to circulate through the local community.

The story of the Melon Heads is a much later addition, but it also concerns Swift's Hollow. At the end of 1903, the mansion was bought by the Reverend Johann Sprunger, a Lutheran minister with the idea of starting a self-sustaining Christian community there. His intention was to provide work in the local area and also provide a refuge for local neglected and abused children. He hoped to teach both boys and girls the benefits of a virtuous life, as well as farming and husbandry techniques. It was not really an orphanage in the conventional sense. Although there were centralized dormitories in the old house, these were mainly used by Christian workers while the neglected boys were billeted in specially built accommodations at the nearby Hughes farm and the girls at the Howard property. He called his new community "Light and Hope Orphanage."

Gore Orphanage Road was originally simply called Gore Road—taking its name not from the sinister custodian of a ghastly orphanage, but probably from a type of skirt, the outline of which resembled the shape of the road. A "gored skirt" is made from a triangular piece of material that is narrow at the waist but wider and more comfortable at the bottom. These skirts were once quite popular in Ohio and may well have given the road its name. The word *Orphanage* was later added to facilitate the institution that the Reverend Spunger had started there.

Even so, disquieting stories were starting to circulate about the Reverend Johann Sprunger. For example, he and his wife Katherina had moved to Ohio from New Berne, Indiana, where they had run a more conventional orphanage that had been destroyed by a mysterious fire in which three small children had died. Rumor said that the Reverend Sprunger was somehow responsible for the blaze. But there were even more unwholesome stories. There were hints that Katherina was actually the Reverend Sprunger's sister, with whom he was having an incestuous relationship, and when they had run the New Berne facility, they had run it as "Brother and Sister Sprunger" Katherina was the daughter of a Lutheran minister—the Reverend Christian P. Sprunger (the same surname as her husband and no explanation was given for this)—and Johann always kept quiet about his own father. Of course there might have been nothing in the rumors, but it created an atmosphere of suspicion about the old place.

Soon, such bits of gossip began to turn into darker tales of neglect, child labor, and abuse. In order to keep food bills down, the Reverend Sprunger bought sick and dying animals from the farms around and made the children eat the diseased flesh. Porridge was boiled in the same pot that was used to wash soiled underwear. There were tales of beatings and other maltreatment. These stores became exposed when several of the children ran away from the community and turned up in Vermillion on the other side of the river bringing with them alarming stories of neglect and a regime bordering on torture. In 1909, Ohio conducted a formal enquiry into the running of the orphanage. Surprisingly, the Reverend Sprunger and his wife admitted most of the charges that were laid against them, however, because the state had no real laws or framework for dealing with orphanages at the time, no real action was taken to improve the plight of the children. The Sprungers were, however, cautioned and the matter was laid to rest.

In 1908, just as the enquiry was getting underway, a tragic and horrific incident occurred 40 miles to the east in the settlement of Collinwood (now a suburb of East Cleveland). More than 176 children at an elementary school were burned or trampled to death in a fire that completely gutted the building. The blaze, it was believed, had been deliberately started by the school janitor—a German-American named Herter (even though he lost four of his own children and was injured trying to save others)—and he was briefly arrested and detained. The main deaths affected children on the second floor of the building who tried to descend a flight of stairs in order to escape as soon as the fire alarm sounded. However, the fire was already taking hold at the foot of the staircase, and some of the children turned and, according to witnesses, tried to make their way to the classroom. Those who were coming down shoved them into the flames below. When they reached the rear exits, the fleeing children found it locked (this was taken as proof that the janitor had been involved in the fire), but when rescuers managed to open the door, they found that it opened inward and the crush of bodies on the other side prevented anyone from getting through to safety. The fire spread quickly through the trapped children, setting their dresses and hair alight.

It was a truly horrifying incident and one that burned itself into the minds and psyches of both survivors and rescuers alike. The disaster meant the end of Collinwood as a settlement, and many of the families, fearful at the lack of fire control there, moved into places like Vermillion, bringing the memory of that horror with them. The horror of the account somehow transferred itself to the Light and Hope Orphanage, and the Gore Road and ghost stories concerning burning babies floating through the air along the orphanage road soon proliferated.

The Reverend Sprunger died in 1911, two years after the state investigation, and the orphanage finally closed in 1916 among a welter of financial problems and unpaid bills. A Pelham Hooker Blossom of Cleveland bought the property, leasing the land to local farmers and the old Swift Mansion was left to rot. Finally, there were a series of fires—perhaps deliberately started by locals—and the buildings were partly destroyed and then pulled down. But the horrifying legends continued.

Stories began to circulate around the area that before its destruction the orphanage had been run by an "Old Man Gore" (who had given his name to the Road—this is not true) and who had mistreated those in his charge. The children eventually turned against him, killing him and burning the buildings down. This is probably some sort of confused memory of the events in Collinwood, a number of miles away, and has little to do with Swift's Hollow.

A more intriguing story concerns a reputed Dr. Crow who allegedly took over the building after it closed. This mysterious figure spells his name Crow, Crowe, Trobaino, Krohe, Kroh, or even Khune and was said to be a scientist conducting experiments on his own behalf or at the behest of the American government. He is invariably portrayed as a sinister figure who used unorthodox methods for obtaining his specimens, all of whom were children. No date was given for the doctor's activities, but it is said to have been around the late 1800s/early 1900s or just after the First World War. The purpose of the experiments is unknown, but it may have involved injecting kidnapped children with fluid, which caused their heads to swell in a grotesque way. The experiments were also supposed to increase their strength and their ferocity, and they eventually turned on Crow and killed him, setting fire to his house (the Gore Orphanage). They then escaped into the surrounding woods where they presumably still live, a group of beings with bulbous heads and wide-staring eyes. They still appear to be aggressive and according to local legend are known to steal away "normal" children for unknown purposes—perhaps for food. A number of people in the Kirtland area claim to have seen the Melon Heads, as they are known, either in gloomy places in the woodlands, or peering through the windows of houses late at night, often terrifying those inside. Of course, there is a recognized medical condition associated with the appearance—hydrocephalus, or "water on the brain," which is an abnormal accumulation of cerebro-spinal fluid in the ventricles or cavities of the brain. This often gives rise to diminished cognitive faculties and a "melon head" appearance in the individual. Some claim that the legends might have been started by some unfortunate hydrocephalic in the area who may have been wandering about. However, there *may* be some truth in the idea.

Researcher Ryan Orvis, citing the *West Geauga Sun* as the source (Geuaga County is near to Kirtland), found evidence of a Dr. Kroh who was in the area around World War II. Kroh was an unlicensed doctor, but a follower of the Austrian priest and geneticist Johann Gregor Mendel (1822–1884) who conducted experiments in plant cross-hybridization. Kroh, it was claimed, attempted to alter the genetics of children by injecting them with various substances. One of his experiments allegedly increased the size of their heads in an attempt to increase their intelligence. The experiments failed and in a fit of scientific pique, Dr. Kroh bundled all his deformed subjects into a car and released them around the area of the Chagrin River Road in Kirtland. There they fled into the woods. In some of the newspaper accounts, Orvis acknowledges, the doctor treated his subjects with radiation, so these mutated children must also have been radioactive. Several other newspaper sources have pointed to the strangely large number of children's graves in nearby King's Memorial Road and suggest that many of these were from Dr. Kroh's failed experiments.

Since the end of World War II, there have been a number of sightings of Melon Heads around Gore Orphanage Road and Wisner Road in the Kirtland suburbs. Most of these have been either the accounts of passing tourists in the area or by local schoolchildren who have been exploring in the woods. A number of them describe the same thing—a humanoid with an abnormally large head, dressed in what seems to be an "institutional" way, namely a torn (and often

bloodstained) white shirt, and brown, ragged, button-up trousers. Maybe, of course, this has more to do with imaginations concerning the orphanage which operated in Swift's Hollow than with Dr. Kroh. For all Ryan Orvis's research and in spite of the newspaper stories, there is no real evidence to connect the Kirtland suburbs with certain abnormal genetic experiments. But that's not to say that they didn't happen!

The strange stories of the cursed family of Joseph Swift, the spiritualism of Nicholas Wilber, and the utter strangeness of the Light and Hope Orphanage of the Reverend Sprunger have all combined to create the creepiness out of which the legend of the Melon Heads has emerged. The region can certainly be spooky and several other local legends have grown up around it—for example, there is a Cry Baby Bridge (common in several areas of Ohio) on Wisner Road, just north of Kirtland's Chardon Road. The ghostly child who weeps there is said to be one of the orphans from the old Gore Orphanage. In such circumstances, it might be easy to dismiss the Melon Heads as an urban myth dreamed up by teenagers and the gullible. But what if there's something more to it? There are similar stories of these beings in other States.

In Michigan, for example, the story of the Melon Heads is told around the old Felt Mansion near Laketown Township. Local legends say that they are descendants of hydrocephalic inmates at the Junction Hospital for the Insane, not too far from the old mansion. As a result of abuse by some of the doctors, they broke out and fled into the woods, and lurk there until the present day. The flaw in this story is that there never was an asylum in the region, although there was a hospital. The Allegan County records simply denote it as a regular hospital with no special facilities for the mentally disturbed. Nevertheless, a local newspaper, *The Holland Sentinel,* carried stories of beings seen in the woods and some people's recollections of the Weeble Heads who were supposed to live there. According to some of the printed stories, several of the doctors were killed by the Melon Heads and their chewed remains lie buried not far from where the old mansion once stood. A spectral sight of one of the doctors being killed was frequently seen through the Felt Mansion door.

In Connecticut, the legend takes on an even darker tone, with its origins supposedly dating back to Colonial times. In Fairfield County, a certain family settled in the Trumbull area, having been driven out of Massachusetts for suspected witchcraft and cannibalism. Faced with hostility from their neighbors, the family, which was a large one, retreated to the woods where inbreeding took place, giving rise to the Melon Head legends of today. The legend has of course been amended to include the now-obligatory insane asylum and the riot by some of the malformed inmates. There may have been a hospital at Grant Wood in the county, which experienced a serious fire late in 1960. It is said that some of the patients who were evacuated disappeared and were never found—these are the ancestors of the present-day Melon Heads. In Trumbull, they supposedly haunt Velvet Street (which is also known as "Dracula Drive") whilst in Shelton, it is Saw Mill City Road, and in Milford on Zion Hill Road. Velvet Street is still an un-paved dirt road running through deep woodlands and several people disappeared along its length. During the recent paving of Saw Mill City Road a few years ago, a number of workers reported hearing voices in the woods calling to each other, but none reported seeing anything. Were these the voices of Melon Heads? Simi-larly, a couple of tree experts, checking the woodlands for a tree fungal infestation, thought they glimpsed a couple of strange figures moving in the undergrowth. The Melon Heads again?

Back at Swift Hollow in Ohio, nothing now remains of Rosedale, the grand mansion that Joseph Swift erected there, apart from a few old graffiti-covered sandstone blocks and a similarly decorated entrance column. There is nothing really to see. However, visitors to the site claim a feeling of being watched in the surrounding woodlands and there are often unexplained calls and noises around the ruin. Maybe the story of the Melon Heads is no more than an urban myth, but it's one that is just about on the edge of believable. If you want to test it, I wouldn't really advise that you go too far into the deep woodlands! You don't know what might be waiting for you there!

Hermitage Castle

The Borders, Scotland

"The evil that men do lives after them."
—William Shakespeare, *Julius Caesar* Act III Scene ii

Perhaps no fortification anywhere in Scotland bears a more sinister reputation than the lonely Hermitage Castle near the town of Hawick in the Scottish Border Country. It stands on a stretch of bleak moorland, which runs down toward the English border in an area that was once driven by fierce conflicts earning it the nickname "gatehouse of the bloodiest valley in Britain," and its grim and severe aspect blends well with that epithet. At one time, the stronghold was one of the most prominent fortresses within the Debateable Lands, an area that stretched between the Scottish and English Borders, but belonged to neither. They were passed between warring factions sometimes becoming Scots, sometimes becoming English, but never really settled. Today the castle is little more than a ruined shell alone on the bleak moorlands with its memories and ghosts.

No one is exactly sure when Hermitage Castle was built or exactly who built it. It is thought, however, that the original fortress was probably a timber affair built around 1240 by Nicholas De Soulis, a Norman knight who had been granted lands in the Scottish Borders. Its purpose was probably to control the area of Liddlesdale, which was especially wild and lawless during border wars between the Scots and the English. It seems to have been little more than a basic Norman castle—what was called a motte and bailey (a stout emplacement above a general military yard)—which was common of many Norman strongholds of the time. Hermitage would remain in the hands of the De Soulis, family until approximately 1320 when an infamous character, William De Soulis, was accused of plotting against the Scottish king of the time, Robert the Bruce. De Soulis was expelled from Court, imprisoned for a time in Dumbarton Castle, and his own castle and lands were taken in forfeit by the Crown.

In the early 1330s, the castle was in the hands of an English noble, Ralph de Neville, who did not enjoy particularly good relations with his Scottish neighbors. It was besieged in 1338 by Sir William Douglas, a local noble from Liddlesdale (known at the Knight of Liddlesdale), who claimed the fortress as his own. Douglas had an ongoing feud with Sir Alexander Ramsay, the Sheriff of nearby Teviotdale. Ramsay had the title of Sheriff conferred on him by the Bruce's son, David II, and the powerful Douglas thought that it should have been his. So, although the two men had been close friends at one time, Douglas ordered Ramsay seized and taken to his newly acquired Hermitage Castle. Here he allowed him to starve to death in its dungeons. His pitiful, emaciated ghost is frequently seen around the ramparts of the castle even today.

In 1353, William Douglas made an unfortunate alliance with the English and was murdered by his own godson for his betrayal. Hermitage was taken over by Hugh De Dacre, who rebuilt the wooden structure in stone, which form the ruins that we can see today. However, De Dacre only held it briefly and it soon passed back into the hands of the Douglases who began to refortify and extend their stronghold. They became the Earls of Angus, powerful Border lords. In the late 1400s, however, Archibald Douglas, the 5th Earl (also known as "Bell the Cat") made a "treacherous treaty" with agents of the English king Henry VII and was ordered by the authorities of King James IV of Scotland to hand over Hermitage Castle in compensation. It was then handed over to the Hepburns, who were the Earls of Bothwell. The most famous of the clan was James Hepburn, the 4th Earl (see Dragsholm Castle, Denmark), who was the third husband of Mary Queen of Scots. The queen briefly visited Hermitage around 1560 on her way to Jedburgh toward the end of her reign while Hepburn was there recovering from a severe injury. However, by this time, it became a far less important border stronghold, and when Mary's son, James VI of Scotland (James I of England), cleared out the Debateable Lands, there was little need for such as castle in the area. By the 1800s, it had become no more than a ruin, although interest in it was generated by the romantic writings of Sir Walter Scot, whose ancestors had, of course, come from the border region.

The main legends—especially the many dark ones—concern the last of the De Soulis line that dwelt at Hermitage. This was William De Soulis, widely known as "the Bad Lord Soulis" or "Terrible William." This was a man who was hated in equal measure by his tenants and by his neighboring lords alike—which is probably the source of the allegations against him by his peers that he was plotting against the king. Reputedly the son of Nicholas De Soulis, who had initially built Hermitage (although some legends state that he was an illegitimate offspring), William was a tyrant and a bully, as well as being extremely arrogant (he once boasted that he should have been the true King of Scotland and not Robert the Bruce, because he was "more fitted." But it got worse. William, the Lord Soulis, was widely suspected of being a Black Magician and of dabbling in the dark arts. It may be that, like many other noble men of the day, De Soulis was experimenting in alchemy (the forerunner of modern chemistry), but this is not certain. His attitude to those around him certainly did not help. It was said that he was involved in human sacrifice and other unspeakable abominations. It was even said that he summoned up the Devil at Hermitage. From the time that he became Lord of the castle in 1318 until he left it in 1320, scores of children disappeared from the locality and it was said that they were being used as sacrifices to dark spirits within the castle walls. It is said that their anguished screams can still be heard echoing around the ruins of Hermitage. De Soulis had a familiar spirit or imp named Robin Redcap that had been given to him by the Devil and it dwelt in Hermitage with him. This familiar was fed on human blood, especially that of virgin girls and children. In return for such offerings, the spirit promised him that

he would be invulnerable to any weapon of steel or iron, and that he could not be bound by anything except a rope of sand.

> *Whilst thou shalt bear a charmed life,*
> *And hold that life of me,*
> *'Gainst arrow, sword and knife*
> *I shall thy warrant be*
> *Nor forged steel nor hempen band*
> *Shall e'er they limbs confine*
> *Till threefold ropes of sifted sand,*
> *Around thy body twine.*

So ran an old verse concerning the Bad Lord, probably taken from a ballad by Sir John Leyden, a popular writer of ballads and friend of Sir Walter Scot. Believing himself to be invulnerable, De Soulis committed even greater atrocities. In a common tale about him, he murdered a local girl—the daughter of a local noble—during one of his frenzied, diabolical rituals, and then also killed her father when he tried to investigate her death. He was only saved from arrest by the intervention of Alexander Armstrong the Lord of Mangerton whom De Soulis later invited to a grand banquet and killed by feeding him poisoned meat. In some other versions of the story, it is Armstrong's own daughter whom De Soulis sexually molested and killed.

This was all getting too much for the Border nobles, and following Armstrong's death, they petitioned King Robert to have him removed. By this time, the king was weary by the ceaseless complaints that he was receiving about De Soulis and is reputed to have said dismissively, "Boil him if you must but let me hear no more of him." This was taken by the Bad Lord's enemies as a royal command to execute him. However, they were well aware of Robin Redcap's magic protecting De Soulis and went to a local magician, Thomas of Ercildoune (often taken to be the celebrated Thomas the Rhymer, who is supposed to have been an actual Scottish poet/magician), to elicit his help. Using certain protections and charms, Thomas managed to bind the Bad Lord with a leaden belt in which a thin strand of fine sand had been hidden. This supposedly rendered De Soulis powerless and he was taken by his captors at Hermitage Castle. But they were not finished with him yet. In order to nullify his powers and to carry out King Robert's instructions, they wrapped him in a single sheet of lead and carried him to the Nine Stane Rig, a great pagan stone circle area two miles to the northeast of Hermitage. There, they prepared a great cauldron and boiled William De Soulis alive.

On a circle o' stanes they placed a pot,
The circle o' stanes but barely nine,
They heated it red and fiery hot
Till its brass did glimmer an' shine
They rolled him up in a sheet o' lead,
A sheet for a funeral pall,
An' they put him doon in the cauldron,
An' they melted him bones an' all.

Of course this may be no more than a gruesome tale of the Border Country, but William De Soulis does seem to disappear from the pages of recorded history after this, so there may be some truth to it.

Although probably dead, the legacy of the Bad Lord Soulis lived on amongst the stones of Hermitage. Although he was gone from the castle, it is said that his familiar Robin Redcap still lurked in the shadows of the place. Redcaps (also known as Dunters or Powters) are a type of malignant fairy in the Border areas. They supposedly resemble little old men with long beards and wizened faces, and are almost vampiric in their ways, subsisting partly on human blood. They are also invariably drawn to evil places, and the wickedness of the Lord De Soulis infested Hermitage Castle with their presence. Indeed, even today, Border folk will say that great numbers of them still hide in the darkness of the castle, ready to attack anyone who ventures too close.

The ghost of the Bad Lord himself, of course, is never far away. His figure, it is said, is frequently seen glowering out across the countryside from the fortress's ruined battlements. Recently, according to several local newspapers, a group of workmen, engaged in some repair work at the castle, are said to have spied a figure looking down on them from one of the high windows where nobody could be (as there are no floors in the upper stories). Lord DeSoulis is also seen at various other points around the castle, always accompanied by the wailings and sobs of children. According to other local legends, the Bad Lord drives up to the castle gate on certain nights of the year (for example, at Halloween) in a carriage made entirely out of human bones and drawn by skeletal horses. Anyone he encounters will be invited to climb into this hideous carriage with him and taken off to the afterlife—and, says local tradition, it is almost impossible to refuse his invitation.

Other ghosts haunt Hermitage as well. One of the most frequently seen is said to be that of James Hepburn, the notorious Earl of Bothwell. His specter is seen dripping blood from an open wound (which he may have received in a battle before he was taken to Hermitage to recover) wandering mournfully about near the gate area. Both the phantom and the blood disappear almost immediately after they are seen. And of course, the phantom of Mary, Queen of Scots, is supposedly often seen in the castle grounds. For a deceased person, she seems to travel quite a bit, as her specter is seen in many other Scottish castles. Yet another ghost, what seems to be a robed and cowled holy man, is sometimes seen in the vicinity of the castle and this may be a remnant of a time before the fortress was built. The word *Hermitage* means a place apart, often a religious retreat, and this may be the specter of some early hermit or monk who has availed himself of the isolated site.

Whatever phantoms prowl there, Hermitage Castle actually *looks* as though it should be haunted. The bleak moorland, the gaunt and forbidding walls, the moving shadows as the sun sets, all contribute to the overall sinister atmosphere of the place. And of course, the evil reputation of the Bad Lord Soulis lends color to the gloomy traditions of the place. Maybe there *is* some ancient and malignant force contained in its stones.

Hexenturm

Heidelberg, Germany

"Denn die Toten reiten schnell."
—Gottfried August Burger, *Lenore*

It is quite easy to experience that sensation of "creepiness" in some old house or in the middle of some ruin or remote place far away from the warmth and security of human companionship and habitation. Loneliness and isolation combined with a sensation of antiquity and decay can, understandably, generate an uneasy feeling in many of us. But what about in the middle of a bustling town? Will the same sensations be generated in the middle of thronging streets or busy shops? Maybe, argue some, that sensation is simply an innate response within us to ancient energies and forces that continually course through the world and can affect us no matter where we are. And who is to say that this is not the case? Further, what if some of the "conduits" or "relay points" for these ancient forces lay in the middle of thriving towns? Would such points give us the feeling of "creepiness" when we passed close to them, even though we were in the middle of a busy street or market place? And how would we explain such a feeling to ourselves?

Such places indeed may well exist—some natural, some man-made. In Germany, it is suggested, some of the man-made structures are stone towers known as Hexenturm (witch's towers). These, it is said, serve as a focus for primal energies in almost the same way as an electricity sub-station, and within their stone walls, supernatural forces seethe and flicker, unseen by human eye, but sometimes detected in other ways by particularly sensitive people. Such places can sometimes produce what we might call "ghost images," especially if they are very old. There are witch towers in a number of German towns such as Coburg, Herborn, Hoffheim Idstein, Marburg, Salzburg in Austria, as well as many more. At Wildensen Castle near Leibertingen, witches burned at the very top of the tower there—although this isn't officially a Hexenturm. Witches towers have also one thing in common—many of them were prisons, though not necessarily for witches. The greater majority of them date from the mid-19th century and were used solely to confine women. Only a few of them are older than this and these have been used to confine (and torture) women who had been suspected of witchcraft.

Although it didn't really get underway until the early 1600s, witch-hunting in Germany was particularly ferocious. This was due to the intervention of the Church and one churchman in particular—Bishop Johann Gottfried von Aschhausen, Prince-Bishop of Wurzburg and Bamburg, who had the dubious nickname "the Witch Bishop." Between 1609 and 1622, he committed more than 300 persons to torture and death, and upon his death in 1622 his successor Johann George II Fuchs von Dornheim maintained the trials and burnings. Among the tortures that were carried out were the boot (a great weight placed on the chest); the hot seat (a roasting hot chair of iron in which the suspect was made to sit); feathers dipped in sulphur applied to various sensitive parts of the body; and scalding hot and ice-cold baths. Many of these inhuman degradations were carried on during the 17th century in the existing Hexenturm. As in many other parts of Europe, a good number of these were muddled old women and young children, all of whom were consigned to the flames. The Prince-Bishop also insisted that many of them were mutilated in degrading ways before this was done.

Although most of the witch towers are comparatively modern, there are still a few that are very old and that may have been used for these purposes. One of the oldest lies in the old town of Heidelberg, in the corner of the market square there. Some will argue this structure is the most potent of all the Hexenturm, where the mysterious forces converge the most freely. The tower, which was originally built in 1392, has now been incorporated into the university of Heidelberg and stands at what was once the Western part of the initial town. This is now a corner of the University courtyard—a pleasant spot that is frequently used by trippers and picnickers. The tower is tall and made of stone, rising over many of the surrounding buildings with six openings in the side that face the courtyard—two large and four small. This, says the legend, was to allow the people to see the execution of local witches. It was certainly used as a prison and torture chamber for medieval sorcerers and malefactors (often women) and, according to some, their evil has somehow leeched into its very stonework. For a structure of its great age, it is remarkably well preserved, perhaps *too* well maintained, it is sometimes argued. Is there something supernatural within the area that keeps it intact?

Heidelberg is an extremely old site. The jawbone of a very ancient prehistoric man—"Homo Heidelberginsis" (Heidelberg Man) dating back between 600,000 and 200,000 years—was found in the nearby village of Mauer in 1907. This makes the area one of the earliest sites of human life in the whole of Europe. Even more significantly, there appears to have been a 5th-century Celtic structure on the Heilingenberg ("The Mount of Saints") a hill on the other side of the River Nekar on which Heidelberg stands. This fortress may have been there from prehistoric times and may have given the town its name. Although many people seem to think that this was some sort of defensive position, there are others who think that it might have been some ritualistic place where sacred but pagan ceremonies may have been carried on. They point to the fact that in early Christian times, a church was erected on this spot as if to "take away the evil influence of the place." This is a place, they say, where ancient gods might have been worshipped in far-off times and their energies still course through the site. This ancient site lies in a form of alignment with the Hexenturm, which serves as a channel for such forces. Was the tower, designed by 14th-century architects, designed specifically for this purpose? Certainly some see the Hexenturm as a kind of Harmonic Convergence Zone—a kind of mystic junction box where a number of lines of force meet and generate their own energies.

So how does all this ancient energy manifest itself? We have already alluded to the feeling of "creepiness," which sometimes assails people when they visit the tower (which is now a national visitor attraction in Heidelberg), but there are other

sensations, too. According to some visitors, another feeling is that of a chilling coldness, which seems to penetrate to the very core of one's being. This is not just a bit of a chill but a real supernatural cold, suggestive of some other world or time.

"When we visited the Hexenturm a couple of years ago," writes an American visitor named Christ on a ghostly experience blogsite, "it was a blisteringly hot day. Europe seemed to have been experiencing a heatwave and it was really hot enough to melt ice cream. However, as we approached the Tower, I began to notice the air begin to chill a little, although none of the others in my group seemed to spot this. And as I drew nearer to the place, the feeling of coldness grew. It wasn't an ordinary chill, the same as you'd get in a freezer, it was a real deep and bone-freezing coldness that seemed to go right into me and made me feel sick. It was as if somebody was reaching inside me with a very cold hand. I had to excuse myself and turn away and although the others were able to visit the site, I was not. I've never been able to explain the feeling to this day."

Was this sensation caused by the ancient power that is said to flow through the tower? Others have experienced similar sensations, some of which have left them ill for a while after. Is the power in the tower similar to some form of ancient radiation that can cause sickness in those who are sensitive enough to experience it?

And the feeling of supernatural and sickening coldness is not the only thing. Some visitors claim to have heard noises—like screams or shouts in the vicinity of the Hexenturm. Some even claim to see figures that have vanished almost as soon as they were glimpsed.

Writing on the same blogsite, another tourist who simply signs herself Katerina says that while visiting the tower, she thought she heard a voice, high-pitched and crying in what she assumed was a form of German (which she herself did not speak). Out of the corner of one eye, she thought she glimpsed a figure off to her right. She couldn't be sure, but it appeared to be that of an old woman clothed in a ragged dress of some kind, which was suggestive of some former time (or so she thought). The figure seemed very stooped and appeared to be limping, holding on to a nearby low wall, as if for support. There was a distinct feeling of evil emanating from the figure, which was not helped by her crippled progress. Thinking it was some sort of beggar-woman or somebody who was ill, she turned but there was nobody there. She looked around but there was nowhere for the old woman to go, even in a hurry. None of her companions had shared the experience, but she says that she too had experienced the chilling cold, although this only lasted, in her case, for a moment.

There have been other experiences, too. Several people walking around the tower have smelled burning, coupled with some other, more sickening odors.

Could it be that they actually smell burning flesh coming from the time when suspected witches were imprisoned and tortured in the Hexenturm? If ancient energy seethes around the place, then it could be argued that they may have the power to evoke the sights and sensations of former years. This may be especially true if that energy force is combined with the strong emotions of the imprisoned and tortured, which have perhaps lain dormant within the very stonework of the old building. Perhaps this would explain the sounds of screaming and weeping.

Another visitor claims that he or she saw a tall man with a longish beard and carrying an unsheathed sword close to the Hexenturm. The man looked rather untidy and was dressed, once again, in clothes more suited to a former era. Thinking that it was part of an historical pageant organized by the university or the town council, the visitor turned to speak and the man melted away, as if he were no more than smoke, and leaving no trace of his presence. He seemed unaware of the visitor or indeed of many of the other people who coursed about the visitor attraction. The visitor also states that although the vision was looking directly ahead, he seemed to be also unaware of his surroundings. Perhaps, some have suggested, he was one of the guards the Hexenturm when it was a prison. Others say that they have seen a lady clad in a long and flowing white dress and with long skirts run across the yard under the tower at certain hours of the night. She appears to be too grandly dressed to have been one of the inmates of the Tower, although it is possible that she may have been incarcerated there at some time. She also appears to be screaming, although no sound is heard. She often runs through a wall close to the tower and vanishes completely.

What is the secret of the Hexenturm? Is it indeed some form of ancient psychic junction box acting as a receptor for ancient energies that flow across the immediate landscape? Or did the terrible imprisonments and tortures that were carried on there long ago leave an indelible mark on the tower—like some old photograph or print? With such an ancient and mysterious structure, who can say?

Houska Castle

Blatce, Czech Republic

"My son I must warn you…Satan's claws are long and the
grave is not always trustworthy."
—Theophile Gautier, *The Dead Leman*

Would you visit a castle that had been constructed over a nest of demons, above caverns that were said to run all the way to the Gates of Hell? I thought not. And yet, if you were to visit Houska Castle in Blatce, near Prague, that's exactly where you'd be. The castle, thought to be one of the most haunted in Europe, if not the world, stands on a rocky hill about 47 kilometres north of the Czech city and is probably one of the best-preserved medieval strongholds anywhere.

The fortress was built during the reign of Ottokar II, King of Bohemia (1253–1276) and was initially thought to have been one of a number of castles constructed to defend his lands from the advances of Bela IV of Hungary. However, that theory can be dismissed, as Houska was built without any proper fortifications, without a water source, without any kitchens, and with no trade routes nearby to defend. At the time of its construction, it was unoccupied. Why, then, was it built? This has always been a question that has dogged historians. It later served as an administration center from which royal estates could be managed, and between the years 1584–1590, further constructions were carried out, turning it into a kind of Renaissance castle, but still keeping the outlines of the original. The fortress was built over a very large cave system which was, according to folklore, one of the Seven Entrances to Hell to be found in the world. There is a very deep pit—so deep that no one has ever been to the bottom of it—directly underneath the castle chapel. Tradition says that Ottokar used convicted criminals as labor in order to construct the fortress, many of whom were killed as soon as the building was finished. However, the monarch also stated that he would grant a pardon to anyone who was lowered into this pit on a rope and report back what he saw. The first man was lowered down but was only gone a few moments when he started screaming wildly and had to be hauled up again. It was found that he had aged more than 30 years—his hair had turned white and his face was covered in wrinkles. His mind was gone and he made no sense, but kept screaming about half-animal, half-human beings who lived down there in the dark, and of winged creatures that flapped about through the blackness. Throughout the years, there are many stories of an alternative world, lying somewhere beneath the Castle (whether it was Hell or not) people have allegedly disappeared within Houska's precincts, never to be seen again, and many people have taken the legends very seriously. Indeed, many people believed that the castle had been built over a tear in reality (the space-time continuum) and was there to prevent beings from another dimension entering our own. Some churchmen taught that it was constructed to prevent demons from issuing forth and polluting our own reality, and that this was why the chapel had been built over the deep pit. Many believed such tales.

One of those believers was Adolph Hitler, who instructed a scientific team to go to the castle to conduct experiments on a possible inter dimensional portal there. A massive file containing details of their findings was returned to Berlin, but has since vanished. During work carried out in the 1960s, three skeletons, thought to be German soldiers dating from the Nazi period, were unearthed in the main yard. At first, it was thought that they had been attacked by something large and fierce, but it later emerged that all three had been executed.

The chapel is a ghostly place with its walls covered in paintings—some of the oldest such art in Europe—depicting demons and slain dragons. There are some other, less identifiable additions to the main pictures, hinting at creatures that defy description. Could these be representations of things that have emerged from the pit beneath the chapel at some point?

And, of course, ghosts abound. One particular specter is a ghostly black horse, headless and with blood gushing from its neck. This has been seen by a number of visitors, especially within the vicinity of the main gates where it seems to run toward the castle wall, leap into the air, and vanish completely.

"We were on our way into dinner," said one visitor, "when there was a sound like a distant galloping—a horse approaching at great speed, perhaps. And we turned to see this massive black shape come hurtling toward us. In a moment and before we could really make out what it was, it was past us. I thought that it was an animal of some kind, a horse maybe, but it seemed to have no head. And then it was gone into the wall and had vanished without a trace. It was all over in less than a minute. I truly don't know what it was." There is no record as to what this spectre might be—a horse killed in battle perhaps which, for some reason, keeps returning? Is it possible that it was a demon?

Other people have claimed to have seen long lines of individuals progressing toward the castle, but chained together as if they were prisoners. Each individual, however, boasts some sort of horrific injury, and some are even said to be carrying their heads. Some have even claimed that a giant black dog—the Devil?—is attacking and biting several people along the length of the chain. There is no explanation for this vision although it does go back to the building of the castle using criminal labor. Many of these sightings have lasted for several minutes and have been witnessed simultaneously by a number of people.

And of course, the chapel seems to be the center of ghostly or demonic activity. Howls, blasphemies, and shrieks have been heard at all hours of the day and night, some coming from underneath the floor, some from the walls around. At one point, a visiting priest saw something squatting on top of the altar, which looked like something midway between a human being and a large frog. "It looked at me very threateningly," said Father Jerzy Zajic. "Its eyes were very red and seemed to hold the fires of Hell. Then it seemed to fade away like a cloud of thick black smoke and there was nothing there. But I could still feel the chill of its presence. I was convinced that it was the Devil or something like it." Other people have felt tugs on their coats in the chapel gloom or have tripped up unexpectedly with nobody there. Some have seen small shadows, which didn't appear to be altogether human, scuttle away into the darkest recesses of the place. These shadows may be another form of life from beyond the veil, or perhaps devils from the underground pit. Voices are regularly heard coming from inside the chapel by workmen outside—sometimes heavy tones like chanting, sometimes sounding a bit crazy, like the chattering of madmen. When the chapel doors are opened, there is, of course, no one inside. According to some traditions, it was in the chapel that the Nazis carried out some of their interdimensional experiments—maybe such testing has called up the past or has released something from another world.

And such presences are not unique to the chapel area, for people have complained of them all through the castle—along the corridors and even in the Knight's Study. While staying in the Hunting Lodge in the grounds of the castle, a lady named Zdena Vrzalava awoke from a relaxing sleep in her room when something loud fell close by. She awoke her husband and together they saw two dark figures in the corner of the room. They seemed to be engaged in some form of conversation and, as Zdena looked at them, they seemed to fade away like shadows. However, she had caught a little of their whispering and she thought that she'd heard the word *murder* amongst it. A chill crept through her, though whether it was a chill from what she'd heard or an actual physical chill from the figures themselves she could not say. The sight of those dark conspirators troubled both her and her husband for many years afterward.

It is said that some of the castle corridors are haunted by the form of a great hound, which can transform itself into a black-robed cowled figure, like a monk. A number of visitors have sought to approach this figure, but when they do, it simply melts away. Some guests in the castle have complained about an unpleasant and overwhelming stench as it does so.

A more traditional ghost sometimes stares down from one of Houska's high windows into the yard below. A woman dressed in white, with dark ringlets falling about her shoulders, stares wistfully out into the night and rubs her hands in a mournful fashion before turning away. She seems to be waiting for somebody in the courtyard below, although who she is or who she waits for is unknown. Many people have seen her and those who have done so have been gripped by a great and terrible sadness. The "White Lady," as she is known, is the more recognizable sort of ghost around Houska, although she certainly has the power to strike fear into all who see her.

Other people have experienced curious phenomenon in the castle—doors will suddenly open and close without warning, mirrors will fall from the walls, chairs will move, and crockery will smash without reason. One guest, Jaromir

Simonek, was having a drink with some friends in a room on the third floor when glasses that had been placed on a table suddenly started moving around of their own volition. They rose high above the table, before the eyes of the astonished company, as though they were being carried round in unseen hands. Finally, they were lowered back to the table again and placed in a different position in the center of the table. There was no explanation for the amazing event, although several of the witnesses blamed the intervention of evil spirits that had come up from the chapel.

The cellars of the castle are dark and gloomy and are known as Satan's Office or as the Devil's Antechamber. There is even a large and ornate chair down there that resembles a throne, though nobody knows who created it or for what purpose. However, it is said that a black-robed and faceless priest appears there from time to time, sitting in the chair and then rising to walk up the stairs before vanishing. What his connection might be to Houska is unknown—perhaps he is someone from the old abbey that once stood on the site. There were rumors that some of the monks there were not exactly as holy as they should have been, and that Black Magic was practiced within its walls. Maybe this is some ancient memory of that time.

A corridor that runs down to Hell; tales of strange and flapping creatures and animalistic entities; a White Lady and a faceless monk; and peculiar Nazi experiments—these are some of the things that give Houska its strange and often overwhelming atmosphere. Does the castle truly stand over a rent in the veil of space and time or is there something even more sinister and more diabolic lurking far below it, waiting to burst through into our own world? It certainly isn't a place to spend a quiet night—especially if you're of a nervous disposition!

Leap Castle

County Offaly, Ireland

"Raised in blood; blood be its portion."
—The Curse of Leap Castle

If, as an old country saying goes, all houses in which men have lived and died are haunted, then maybe some places are more haunted than others. Buildings with a long and dark history or where barbaric acts have taken place are perhaps more likely to hold an aura of supernatural danger about them than others. And in Irish folklore, it is also widely believed that an already-haunted building will often attract other phantoms and ghostly beings, drawn to it like moths to a jaundiced flame. Even certain items that are found within the building might draw ghostly and unwelcome entities to a place—the unwashed clothes of a "scandalous" woman for instance, human bones from a person who died before their time, religious artifacts that have been stolen or misappropriated, the stain of blood spilled in anger, or even moldy food or dirty crockery all hold a supernatural attraction. Understandably in this list, it is the idea of spilled blood or human bones that can often draw down (or be used to draw down) the most dangerous of all the phantoms which prowl the spiritual outer reaches.

Not only this, but the site where a house is built can often affect the type of spirits that is drawn to it. A house built on the site of a graveyard (or even of an unmarked grave) will undoubtedly be a troublesome place, but so can buildings constructed on the sites of prehistoric tumuli, of old churches or monasteries, or ancient hospitals or workhouses. The spirits of former residents or inmates can sometimes linger on and bring similar beings to them. And where very ancient structures are built upon, very ancient forces can sometimes be retained in the very earth and stones of the site. When looking at an allegedly "creepy house," great attention must be given to both its situation and its history. No dwelling exemplifies this notion more than Leap Castle, built on the borders between County Offaly and North Tipperary in Ireland.

The casual passer-by on the road between Birr and Kinnity might miss Leap Castle, lying deep in a small valley surrounded by dark trees. Situated just beyond the present-day village of Clareen, it once guarded a strategic trade route through the frowning Slieve Bloom Mountains, which connected the coast with the plains of Leix and Offaly. During the unsettled 15th and 16th centuries, routes such as this were fought over by various factions who sought to control trade in the region and used for military purposes. The area around the Slieve Bloom was often a bloody battlefield, just the place to lure dark creatures from the beyond. But there was something else—something that was even older.

A little way along the road from Clareen lies what remains of Seir Kieran, long regarded as one of the oldest Christian sites in Ireland. It is said to date from AD 401 which would put it roughly 50 years before the arrival of St. Patrick in Ireland, and it is dedicated to the obscure holy man St. Kieran the Elder (or Ciaran of Saigir, not to be confused with St. Kieran, the founder of Clonmacnoise). Before the holy man set up his hermitage there, however, the site was probably an important pagan earthwork, which dates back to the Iron Age. It may have been a ritual centre in the ancient Kingdom of Osraige, which would later be incorporated into the Kingdom of Ossory, and may well have been a place where the druids practiced. There are even suggestions that human sacrifice might have been carried on there. In many minds, the place was a concentration of dark and pagan forces, which were not entirely dissipated with the coming of the Christians. Indeed, some of the "ghosts" that prowl the countryside around Leap are "elemental powers" that have been stirred up by the latter partial destruction of the ancient earthwork. One of these is supposed to lurk around the main staircase of the tower-house—an eerie, twisting climb—ready to attack the unwary who are making their way to the higher levels of the castle.

On one of my last trips down there, I stopped at a little roadside shop at the village of Clareen. There is much reverence for the ancient earthwork in the village where nearly every family names a son Kieran in honor of the saint who made his hermitage there. But there seems to be a fear of the place as well.

"When they cut up that earthworks to build churches and castles" the old lady behind the counter told me when I asked her about Seir Kieran, "they let all manner of pagan things loose. Things that had been sleepin' there for thousands o' years rose up to wander the world again. Some of them are up in the castle—I've heard that often ever since I was a girl."

The first "overlord" of the area was the Norman knight Theobald Fitzwalter who destroyed much of the earthwork by building a motte and bailey on the site, but who also "encouraged and developed" some of the Irish clans in his domain, many of whom took quasi-Norman names such as O'Carrig, Fanning, Lawless, Purcell, and O'Bannion. Important though these clans were, it was another, more ferocious sept that really left its mark on the area. They were the O'Carrolls— "the dark princes of Ely," a name by which that portion of Offaly was originally known.

The O'Carrolls were a northern clan—possibly from the present-day Border area around Tyrone, Monaghan, and the Slieve Beigh Mountains—who had been pushed south by a massive expansion of the O'Neills in Ulster. Reputedly tracing their lineage back to Cearbeall, a 9th-century Irish king, they were described as a "lordly and princely sept." As settlers they were savage, subduing all the indigenous clans and seizing large tracts of land for themselves. As the territory in the Kingdom of Ely was excellent land, lying as it did on the edge of the Golden Vale in Tipperary, the clan prospered and expanded, soon controlling an important area and establishing themselves as princes of the entire region. In order to defend these estates, they built Leap Castle, once described by the Earl of Desmond, as "one of the most strategic and best defended fortresses in the Irish Midlands" in the late 15th century.

The name *Leap* is puzzling, but local folklore puts it down to a rather gruesome legend. The full name of the site is Leim Ui Bhannain or the Leap of O'Bannion, and tradition states that when the O'Carrolls seized the land, the O'Bannions were the indigenous clan. They refused to pay tribute to their new overlords, and to resolve the dispute, the O'Carrolls made them a surprising offer. On the newly acquired lands, two great pieces of rock rose out of the ground near the old earthen fort. If an O'Bannion champion could leap between these two rocks and land safely, the clan would be excused their tribute, but if the champion fell, the O'Bannions must accept the O'Carrolls as their masters.

The feat was agreed and an O'Bannion champion came forward, only to miss the leap and be dashed to pieces on the ground below. The O'Carrolls then turned on the O'Bannions, slaughtering many of their best men, seizing their lands and building a number of fortifications there. In a macabre addition, it is said that they used some of the O'Bannion champion's blood to mix the mortar for the foundation stones of the castle on the spot where he'd met his end. This gave rise to a terrible curse, which hangs over the place today: "Raised in blood, blood be its portion."

Whether or not this story is true, Leap was built around the late 1470s by Mulroney O'Carroll, possibly on the site of an old O'Bannon fortress. And if there is a curse, then it affected the O'Carrolls from the time the castle was raised. Some of those born there were mentally deficient; others died from what the chroniclers call "the creeping plague," a strange unspecified disease that took its victims to a slow and lingering death. In 1489, John O'Carroll died "most horribly" at Leap from an ailment referred to in the records as the "bloody flux and a pox." Was it the curse of the dead O'Bannions, or something that had arisen out of the destroyed prehistoric earthworks at Seir Kieran?

Much of Leap's sinister reputation arose out of the turbulent 16th century. Ely O'Carroll, as the area was now called, had become an important "buffer zone" between the English-backed Dukes of Ormond and North Tipperary—the Butlers—and the Fitzgerald Earls of Desmond and Kildare, whose conflict tore through the Irish Midlands. Families were torn in their loyalties between the two factions—none more so than the O'Carrolls. And in these bloody times, Leap Castle took on an even greater strategic significance.

In 1541, following a period of intense fighting, Leap passed into the hands of Tadhg Coach O'Carroll, known as One-Eyed Tadhg. He was, however, not the eldest of his immediate family and was therefore not the obvious heir to Ely. He was also already at war with his cousin Calvagh O'Carroll over territorial matters, and he had at least two elder brothers who should have taken precedence over him. The eldest, John O'Carroll, was weak-minded and was therefore unfit to lead the clan, while Thaddeus McFir was considered incapable of the necessary ruthless leadership because he was a priest. Nevertheless, Thaddeus had formed an alliance with the powerful Earls of Desmond and despite his Holy Orders, was well-skilled in politics and devious dealings. His dabblings in the political field often brought him into conflict with his younger brother Tadhg.

Tadhg ruled his domain with an iron fist, murdering all those who opposed him. As a prospective ruler in Ely, he sought to extend the border of the Kingdom through a program of slaughter and burning. He created treaties with James the Lame, Duke of Ormond, in order to gain Butler support for his murderous activities. Meanwhile, his brother Thaddeus had been negotiating with the opposing Fitzgerald faction and was undermining Tadhg at every turn, a dangerous thing to do. Tadhg decided enough was enough and that his brother would have to die. He nonetheless invited Thaddeus to use the chapel at Leap as his own personal religious sanctuary.

The chapel at Leap still lies at the very top of the central tower and is accessed by the winding stone staircase. It is small for a chapel, but is isolated, and would have been ideal for prayer and reflection. Tadhg, however, had other plans and, as his brother knelt in prayer at the altar rail, Tadhg crept into the chapel and slit his throat. Although this was an act of murder, it was also an act of blasphemy (to kill a man whilst he was talking to God) and it ensured the total damnation of One-Eyed Tadhg O'Carroll.

With Thaddeus dead, Tadhg's excesses became even more horrendous. He embarked upon a program of unparalleled killing and pillage. So much so that one of the local clans—the O'Mahons (who had supported his brother)—commenced all-out war against him.

During a lull in hostilities, Tadhg made overtures of peace by inviting about 40 O'Mahon clan-members to a grand banquet in Leap Castle. Of course, he had no intentions of allowing them to leave alive. The food and the wine he gave them were all drugged and, as the O'Mahons succumbed to the effects, Tadhg had them carried one by one to the chapel.

There, in the chapel wall, Tadhg had built a long, vertical shaft known as an oubliette, almost like a dumbwaiter, which dropped steeply all the way down to the bottom of the castle. The name comes from the French *oublier* (to forget) and prisoners were hurled into this shaft, which was then bricked up, and they were forgotten about. Tadhg had also lined the sides of the oubliette with metal spikes. It is said that those O'Mahons who remained conscious asked to be thrown down head first, hoping to break their necks rather than die slowly on the spikes. The oubliette remained sealed until the mid-1920s, when it was finally excavated and four cartloads of human remains—perhaps all that was left of the O'Mahon clan—were taken away.

As Tadhg seized more and more lands, extending the boundaries of Ely O'Carroll, the English in Dublin became increasingly alarmed. They sent a large army under the command of Edmund Fahy to curb his power. Fahy was unfortunately betrayed by his allies and was forced to face Tadhg's fury with only a skeleton army. He was comprehensively defeated at Carrigahorrig on the Shannon, and in retaliation, Tadhg burned several towns that were sheltering his troops, including Nenagh, and took scores of prisoners. Back at Leap, he had constructed a massive network of underground dungeons stretching for miles under the countryside. Into these he put the prisoners, sealing them in lightless tombs and leaving them to rot without food in the dark. That network is still there and the cells remain bricked up and unopened, and access to many of them is virtually impassable. Only rats come and go at will.

In 1552, Tadhg made peace with the English and accepted a knighthood, but internal disputes among the O'Carrolls continued to rage. In securing an English title for himself, Tadhg incurred the enmity of his surviving brothers. They approached an old enemy, Calvagh, who, with their urging, entered Leap through a secret tunnel (the location of which has since been lost) and murdered Tadhg as he dozed by the fire. Tadhg died in 1553, bringing an end to his bloody lordship. In 1688, the O'Carroll clan finally left the area in return for a grant of 60,000 acres in Maryland, America. Their ancestral lands became part of the English Plantation, but even then, the dark history of Leap Castle wasn't finished.

Another bizarre and colorful character now became master of the castle. Jonathan Darby, known as "the Wild Captain," was a strong Royalist of eccentric and immoral habits. He had strengthened his claim on the area around the Slieve Bloom Mountains by marrying an O'Carroll princess, but it is said that he greatly abused his wife, his servants, and his tenants alike. Wild and orgiastic parties were held at Leap as Darby's name became infamous throughout the region.

One of the stories about him concerned a fortune of gold and precious stones that he had somehow amassed. He hid this fortune in a secret chamber somewhere in the castle (which has never been found), the wealth being transported by two servants whom he subsequently killed, bricking their bodies up in the castle walls. (There may be something to this legend, because in the 1960s when some renovation work was being carried out, two skeletons were found behind plaster in one of the chambers.) Sometime afterward, however, he was arrested and accused (falsely, as it turned out) of plotting against King Charles II and was imprisoned in Dublin. When released, many years later, he was on the edge of madness and had completely forgotten where he hid the treasure. It has never been discovered to this day.

The Darbys remained at Leap right up until 1922. They had made many additions to the original O'Carroll fortress, building on Gothic wings and additional rooms. However, with the Irish Civil War raging around them, they moved out and returned to England becoming absentee landlords. The newer Darby additions to the castle were mostly burned by the I.R.A. during the conflict, and today it is partly a ruin. Although the family still retained a connection to the castle, they had gradually sold off the lands in order to meet their bills and became less and less involved in the area. In 1935, Jonathan C. Darby sold his last remaining portion (a little more than 1 acre—it had been 4,367 acres in 1880) to the Irish Land Commission, and ushered in a number of other owners of the burnt-out shell.

Leap Castle has passed through many hands, but is currently owned by the musician Sean Ryan and his wife Anne, who are in the process of rebuilding and restoring the burnt-out wings. The ghosts, however, haven't gone away, and the couple tell many stories of the place. They draw attention to an article written by Mildred Darby, then mistress of the castle, for *The Occult Review* in 1909 in which she talks about encountering the elemental in a gallery between the staircase and one of the bedrooms. The thing touched her and she described it as being a roughly human shape, like a rotting cadaver with a stench like that of rotting carrion.

And in the Bloody Chapel where Thaddeus O'Carroll was murdered, the ghost of his brother and killer Tadhg still prowls. He is now a vampire that attacks all those who enter the burned and ruined chapel to suck their blood. On dark nights between the hours of midnight and one o'clock, an eerie light is said to glow from the glassless window of the chapel to signal his presence there. It is a brave or foolhardy person who will venture there.

And Sean recounts a number of ghost stories as well. The largest bedroom in Leap—known as the State Bedroom—is haunted by the ghost of an O'Carroll princess who has wakened both him and his wife and some of their guests who have slept there. And, when much younger, his daughter Ciara had played with the ghosts of two children who haunt the upper rooms. In fact, a former resident of the gate lodge frequently spoke of two small girls dressed in Victorian clothes who played in front of the castle in the moonlight. One appeared to be lame and it is thought that she had fallen from the tower in some former time. Other guests have seen a man-like figure with what looked like the skull of a sheep as its head, a shaggy black-furred body and great paw-like hands. Sean has seen the ghost of the priest passing through the great hall when he has been working there. The castle is now regarded as one of the most haunted in Western Europe and psychics from as far away as Mexico and Japan have been there to test the eerie atmosphere.

In June 2002, I made one of my visits to Leap to take part in a program for the RTE *Townlands* series. With a TV crew, I sat by the fire in the castle's great hall, while Sean regaled us with stories of the place's macabre history. Just before midnight, I climbed the stone stairs to the Bloody Chapel to see if I could discern the vampiric ghost of Tadhg O'Carroll. Alas, I found nothing there except a great white owl, which had been nesting in the ruin.

The following day, however, we tried to explore some of the underground dungeons that extended for miles around the Castle. Many of the passages were impassable, and many of the cells had been blocked since the 16th century. Rats, some as big as hedgehogs, were everywhere. Even with lights, we couldn't progress very far, but as we were turning back, there was a distinct sound, like a cry from way back in the darkness. It may have been the wind, but it certainly sounded like a scream, and I thought of the remnants of Edmund Fahy's troops who had been sealed up in this fearsome underworld by Tadhg O'Carroll and left to go mad.

Back in the Bloody Chapel, I was standing in front of the oubliette, doing a piece to camera, when I suddenly felt a touch, like that of an incredibly cold hand on the base of my spine. In a moment, the sensation had vanished but there was no doubt that I'd experienced it. Of course, it might have been a chilling gust of air through the glassless windows, but there was no wind that day. As I went to look out over the high window of the chapel, I felt the momentary urge to throw myself from the height into the ruins below, and I wondered if the child who was supposed to have "fallen" from an upper window had experienced the same impulse.

There were other things as we worked—electrical equipment inexplicably failing and restarting, a number of small items going missing, and the sound engineer picking up odd noises—voices, as if people were talking when there was nobody there, and the unmistakable sound of something being dragged across the floor, when there was nothing to be seen. All in all, I was glad to leave Leap Castle behind me, especially when I heard that the night after we'd gone, the eerie light occasionally seen in the Bloody Chapel was said to be burning as brightly as ever.

Do ghosts still frequent the gloomy corridors of Leap Castle? Or like many other great Irish houses, does it owe its sinister reputation to its troubled history? And can anything cleanse the place of the allegedly dark forces that have lurked there? Who truly knows?

Loftus Hall

Wexford, Ireland

"I came on a great house in the middle of the night,
Its open lighted doorway and its windows all alight,
And all my friends were there and made me welcome too,
But I woke in an old ruin that the winds howled through."
—W.B. Yeats, *The Curse of Cromwell*

Standing amidst a desolate landscape in the isolated Hook Peninsula of County Wexford, Loftus Hall is certainly reminiscent of the grandeur of a bygone age. A structure of ivy-covered, grey stone walls, a forest of chimneys, and seemingly endless rows of dark windows, it seems to suggest both a vanished opulence and a sinister, brooding menace. This ancient house is supposed to have once played host to the Devil, and perhaps some vestige of that unholy visitation still lingers in the crumbling stonework of the building.

The original house was built on the site sometime in the 13th century as a residence for the Redmond family. The lands did not prosper greatly under their domination, although they appear to have been reasonable masters. They eventually lost their lands under the Cromwellian redistribution of lands in Ireland—it was claimed that Alexander Redmond had led detachments of troops against Crowell's forces in 1649. They appealed the sequestration of their properties and were given lands in North Wexford in 1684. In 1666, under lands given in the Restoration of the English King Charles II, the Loftus family acquired it and placed their name upon it to reflect their ownership of the estate. The present hall dates from the 1870s, and although it is still privately owned and is not open to the public, it is clearly visible from the twisting road that winds through the Hook Peninsula. However, a plaque on one of the gateposts provides information regarding a strange and terrifying event that happened in its more recent history. It simply details "the ghost story—strange events which happened here in the early 18th century" and this refers to the "visitation of the Devil" to torment the inhabitants of the house.

These were Charles Tottenham and his family, descendants of the Marquis of Ely, who came to live there in the middle of the 18th century. Tottenham's first wife had been the Honourable Anne Loftus and the house was her ancestral seat, which he had inherited. He now came here with his second wife and Anne, his daughter by the earlier marriage. There are two versions of the story, both leading to the same ending and the listener can take whatever one he or she wishes. One is that while they were staying there, a ferocious storm swept across the Hook Peninsula and the seas all around became quite dangerous. The storm lasted for several days, and one night, a mysterious ship of no known origin, was wrecked on the rocks below the Hall. Only one person survived: an elegant young man dressed in expensive clothes. According to some versions of the story, he introduced himself as Joseph Woodley, an English merchant on his way home after being in America. However, he seemed very evasive about the nature of his business or what exactly he had been doing abroad. He stayed at Loftus Hall for a few days, and, as he was a particularly handsome young man, Anne soon took an interest in him.

One night as the wind rattled about the old house and howled like a banshee down the chimney, Charles Tottenham suggested that they should have a game of cards with their new guest in order to pass the time. They drew up a table in front of the roaring fire and Charles began to deal the cards.

In the second version of the story, the wreck does not occur and no young man is saved from it. However, as the storm lashed the building, the wind tugging at the blaze in the hearth, there was a fierce hammering at the door of the Hall. When the servants opened it, they found a stranger in a heavy traveling cloak with his hat pulled down across his face, standing there in the thunderous rain. He explained that his horse had thrown a shoe on the road and under the ancient Irish laws of hospitality, he asked for shelter. This could not be refused, and he was brought in to the fire. He suggested that he might go on as soon as he had warmed himself at the fire and seek out a local blacksmith who might reshoe his horse that night. Charles Tottenham kindly said that this was unlikely, as the blacksmith would be abed; that this was no night for man or beast to be out, and that he was welcome to stay the night at Loftus Hall. Gratefully, the stranger accepted and removed his hat, showing a handsome face that perked Anne's interest. He was given a mug of ale and some dry clothes and settled down by the fire.

It's here that the stories converge for both speak of the game progressing with the handsome visitor winning a number of card games. During the course of the game, Anne accidentally dropped one of her cards on the stone in front of the fire and bent down from her seat to retrieve it. As she did so, she happened to glance at their visitor's feet. Instead of the top boots which he had been wearing, she saw a cloven hoof like that of a beast! And as she looked at it, she suddenly realized just who their guest actually was—the Devil himself come from Hell! The same story—the handsome stranger, the fallen card or some other dropped possession, which reveals the fiend through the glimpse of a cloven hoof—is common in other parts of Ireland from Kerry to Donegal, but the particular version referring to Loftus Hall has a special resonance to it. Rising with a scream, the girl revealed what she'd seen and all heads turned toward their visitor. He rose and his face was like that of a feral animal. Charles Tottenham stood up and made the sign of the cross in the air, calling on the name of Jesus to banish the demon. As if in response, the wind roared around the aged walls of the hall with an even greater ferocity and pulled at the flames of the fire from the chimney. The visitor stood for a moment as though transfixed and then with a growl, he suddenly disappeared in a flash of stinking, sulphurous smoke, which, in turn, vanished into the ceiling.

The family breathed a sigh of relief, but their ordeal wasn't over yet—in fact, it was only beginning. From then on there were a number of very strange and eerie occurrences throughout the hall, which were suggestive of diabolic activity. Live coals leapt from the fire of their own accord; water that had been stored in the pantry turned black like ink, pictures fell from the walls, but didn't break; voices were heard calling softly along certain of the corridors, and some of the rooms became exceptionally cold. It was clear that the Devil, or whatever evil spirit it was, hadn't exactly left the hall. The maids and some of the guests began to complain about being physically pinched and nipped and about having bed-clothes pulled off them as they slept. Charles Tottenham decided that things were getting out of control and that he would have to have the place exorcised in order to drive the spirit out. And he knew just the man to do it.

The majority of exorcisms in Ireland have gone unrecorded. In fact, it was not until after the William Friedkin film of William Peter Blatty's *The Exorcist* in 1973 that Ireland, like the rest of the world, began to take a serious interest in the demonic. Since then, a number of books have appeared detailing various exorcisms in parts of the country, but dating mainly from the 1970s right up to the 1990s. This is not to say, however, that there weren't exorcisms and exorcists before then. In fact, the first reference that we have to an Irish exorcist is to St. Ambrose O'Coffey, who was a noted fighter against demon kind, and who died at St. Columcille's Seat in Magilligan, North Derry in 1187. He was supposed to have left behind several parchments of exorcisms—known as the Druid Library—which were retained at the monastery until its destruction in 1203. The place where the monastery stood in Duncrun, Magilligan is now overgrown and covered in thick brambles, but is an incredibly sinister place—perhaps an abode of spirits drawn by the now-lost ancient scrolls—and worthy of an article in its own right. Another exorcism was carried out by a retired priest named Father Judge near the village of Blacklion in County Cavan at the end of the 1800s and a celebrated exorcism in Coneen, County Fermanagh and the beginning of the 1900s. There were, however, a number of mainly unrecorded local exorcisms (particularly of allegedly haunted houses) in various locations. Whether or not a local priest had been trained as an exorcist, he was frequently called in to deal with unquiet spirits as a representative of the church.

The man that Charles Tottenham had in mind to perform the exorcism was Father Thomas Broaders, who not only was a local clergyman, but was also one of his tenants. Broaders was supposed to be a very holy man and, although it is not clear if this is true, may have had previous experience in "cleansing houses" in the locality. The priest came readily to the Hall. Setting up in one of the rooms where paranormal activity had gone on, he conducted a mass and began to pray for those who had died in Loftus Hall in the past. As he did so, a great wind arose making the windows in the old building shake and rattle. Burning coals leapt out of the fire and the priest was pelted with potatoes from a bin in the kitchen. Nevertheless, he kept up his prayers. A spirit appeared in the form of a small, ragged boy who spat iron nails from his mouth. Father Broaders, however, refused to be distracted and kept praying, asking for Divine help. The wind shrieked around the hall like a host of demons, and the sweat stood on Thomas Broaders forehead,

but he still kept praying and offering up the Holy Sacrament. It was a real battle of wills between the priest and the demonic force. In the end, it was the clergyman who won, because suddenly there was a mighty clap of thunder and a flash of lightning directly above Loftus Hall, and the strange phenomenon suddenly ceased while the feeling of oppression that had latterly characterized the house, lifted. The Devil, it seemed, was gone. There seem to have been few supernatural incidents afterward, although the ghost of a young lady, thought to be Anne Tottenham, was said to appear in the Tapestry Room of the Hall until it was pulled down in 1871 and the new Hall was built.

After the terrible exorcism at the Hall, Thomas Broaders continued as a priest in the locality. Indeed he became the parish priest of the Hook and Ramsgrange areas and continued in that role for the next 50 years. He was much loved and well-respected and when he died in 1773, he was laid to rest in Horetown Cemetery where his epitaph reads:

> *"Here lies the body of Thomas Broaders,*
> *Who did good and prayed for all*
> *And banished the Devil from Loftus Hall"*

In 2008, with the Tottenham family now living in Canada, Loftus Hall was sold. Although there has been much curiosity and speculation, the identity of the buyer has never been revealed. Loftus Hall remains locked, and while it is in severe need of refurbishment, its new owner has never made any attempt to make even the slightest of repairs. A new film named *Loftus Hall* starring Samantha Mumba (of *The Time Machine* fame) has, however, been announced, although no release date has been specified for it—possibly late 2011. This will be a modern horror film based on the events at the hall.

And of course there are those who say that Thomas Broaders exorcism wasn't completely successful, and that some residue of the diabolic visitation still lingers in the house. Voices, they say, are still heard along the corridors, and strange shadows come and go among the empty rooms. As I stood on the road and looked out toward the grim pile across the desolate landscape, I wondered if something was looking back at me from beyond the distant, dark windows of the place, and although the evening was quite warm, I couldn't suppress a shudder.

Recently, it would appear that Loftus Hall is once again up for sale with an asking price starting at 1,000,000 Euros. Knowing its history, might *you* be interested?

Montpelier House

Dublin, Ireland

"A place of wicked reputation...the very stones ooze evil."
—Fitzjames O'Brien describing Montpelier House

The house stands on Montpelier Hill, a remote place on the very outskirts of Dublin City. Raised high above the Liffey, it looks north over the city ands away toward the plains of Meath and Kildare. The building is now no more than a grey stone ruin, little more than a shell, its walls covered in lichen, slime, and diseased-looking ivy. It seems to ooze malevolence from its very stones, filling anyone who ventures close with a distinct sense of unease.

The house was built in 1725 by the Right Honourable William Conolly, Speaker of the Irish House of Commons who was rumored to be the wealthiest man in Ireland at the time of his death in 1729. He took a great liking to the bleak hillside with its panoramic views and decided to build a retreat there for himself, even though the area was already the focus of much local superstition. The hill, according to the Irish historian and writer Patrick Healy, is referred to as Suide Ui Ceallaig, a fortress of the O'Kellys in the Crede Mihi, the 12th-century diocesan register of the Bishops of Dublin, and contained an ancient earthworks and stone circle that was said to date from prehistoric times. There was a passage grave with a large cairn there too, and traces of these are still visible behind the house. All these ancient remains had a very sinister reputation in the local community. It had been, historians said, a place of Druid worship and a site where ancient pagan gods might still be called down. This was a place where fairies and the spirits of the dead would gather on certain nights of the year and such things were not to be touched, or so local tradition held. Conolly, of course, had no time for "such nonsense" and began to clear away all the megalithic monuments from the hilltop. Shortly afterward, a terrible storm erupted over Dublin and an entire slate roof of the new lodge was blown off. For a number of days afterward, several people spoke of strange appearances within the vicinity of the hill—appearances that vanished as soon as they were seen. Some said that it was the work of the Devil, others that it was the old gods taking vengeance on men for their impropriety, others still that it was the spirits of the dead—those who had raised those monuments—giving voice to their anger. Such stories, of course, made no impression on Conolly, and undeterred, he ordered the construction of a new arched roof—its stone keyed together like a bridge. It was a tremendous feat, the like of which had never been seen in Ireland. In fact, according to Weston St. Joyce, writing in his *The Neighbourhood of Dublin,* published in 1912, it was: "…of such impregnable strength that it has effectually withstood the efforts of wind or devil from that day to this." Building of the lodge continued apace, with Conolly actually using the stones from the cairn and the megaliths to complete it. However, it was noted that, after the lodge was constructed, he did not use it much as a residence—he had other properties in Celbridge, County Kildare, County Meath, and County Londonderry—and even though he was a great skeptic, he always claimed to feel "uncomfortable" when staying in Montpelier (as he named the place). There was something "not quite right about the place," he sometimes confided.

Following the death of Conolly, the lease property passed into the hands of the aristocrat Richard Parsons, 1st Earl of Rosse (although the actual ownership still remained in the hands of the Conolly family), and it is here that the dark reputation of Montpelier *really* begins. Parsons was a bit of a dandy, but he also considered himself to be something of a "sorcerer" and a dabbler in ancient mysteries and Black Magic. Perhaps the pagan tradition of Montpelier appealed to him, and he saw it as the focus of ancient and malign powers. He also headed a group of jaded aristocrats who shared the same dubious tastes and interests as himself. This was the notorious Dublin "Hell Fire Club" and they would certainly leave their mark on the old house and also on the surrounding area. It's not certain whether the Club actually paid money for the actual lease—by a strange twist of fate, William Conolly had purchased Montpelier from Philip Wharton, the 1st Duke of Wharton (1698–1731), who was a notorious libertine, rake, alcoholic, and dabbler in the occult, and is credited with founding the first Hell Fire Club in England between 1719 and 1721. (Some historians dispute this and say that Wharton, although a dissolute character, was only peripherally involved in one of two aristocratic gangs in London at the time—"The Blazing Bucks" and the "Hell Fires"—namely the latter.) However, the Dublin Hell Fire Club took on an especially occult significance. The Club was founded by Parsons and Colonel Jack St. Ledger around 1735. Its members included Lord Santry (who was tried and convicted of murder in 1735); Harry Barry, who was a notorious drunk and womaniser, Colonels Richard St. George, Henry Bessborough and Colonel Clements (several of whom had been accused of bestiality with an ape); as well as Simon Luttrel, Lord Imham of Luttrelstown (described as "the most evil man in Ireland" and "King of Hell"). Although most of their meetings took place at the Eagle Tavern on Cork Hill near Dublin Castle or at Daly's Club—a rather bohemian gentleman's club that was often frequented by radicals and politicians—beside College Green, they used Montpelier House for their more blasphemous revels. Much of these were concerned with trying to raise the Devil or the casting of evil spells and the isolation of the building made it a perfect place for such debaucheries or for the celebration of the Black Mass, which was frequently carried out there. This was a parody of a Christian Catholic Mass, often carried out by an unfrocked priest and involving some sort of sacrifice. Blasphemous books were read in an attempt to summon up evil spirits (according to some they were successful), and there was a lot of drinking and lewd behavior. A chair was left vacant at every meeting as an invitation for the Evil One to join them, and records show that the tipple of choice was scaltheen, a sometimes flaming mixture of hot butter and whiskey. Indeed, so strongly was the connection to the Club that the

building itself is still sometimes known as "The Hell Fire Club" to this day. A painting showing some of the notables of the Club by the artist James Worsdale now hangs in the National Gallery of Ireland and depicts members of the great landed families of both England and Ireland.

In 1740, the "Principle" of the Club was Richard Chapell Whaley, a man who was feared and detested by most of Dublin and by the native Irish in equal measure. He was a direct descendant of Oliver Cromwell, which of course did not endear him much to Irish hearts. Under his leadership, the Hell Fire Club began to plumb new depths. Although they had been content to sacrifice a few black cats from time to time (the black cat was the symbol of the Club, and, in one story, a priest is said to have interrupted one of their masses. Seizing the cat that had been sacrificed on the altar, he uttered an exorcism and a demon shot from the creature's corpse and into the ceiling, bringing down plaster on the assembled throng) they now ventured into the area of human sacrifice. A number of children vanished in the area, never to be found, and there is a story that a mentally deficient dwarf was sacrificed on a makeshift High Altar at Montpelier. But the debauchery did not end there. The Hell Fire Club had an extremely strong Protestant element in it, and many of the rites that they followed mocked those of the Catholic Church. Whaley now suggested that they ride around the countryside, setting fire to the thatched roofs of Catholic chapels, burning worshippers out. This they did, considering it "great sport," and it earned their principle the nickname of "Burn the Chapel Whaley," a name that he held with great relish.

The notoriety of the Hellfire Club was now spreading into folklore and literature. Possibly greatly exaggerated accounts of their excesses were published in several pamphlets circulating in Dublin and eventually found their way into Robert Chambers's *Book of Days* (1864), but lurid stories concerning the Club's activities were also published in *The Gentleman's Magazine* between 1731 and 1736 to the horror of respectable Dublin life. Stories concerned the heir playing cards with a wild stranger and dropping some money. When a member stooped to lift it, they glimpsed the cloven foot of the Devil under the table. Simon Luttrel Lord Imham and 1st Earl of Carhampton, a member of the club, supposedly sold his soul to the Devil in exchange for the Infernal One clearing all his debts. When the Devil came to Montpelier House in order to collect his payment, Luttrel distracted him and fled. However, the same stories are told in various parts of Ireland about unpopular landlords including most notably Dr. Alexander Colville of Galgorm Castle, County Antrim. Stories of such wild excesses were having an effect on Dublin society.

So wild were these stories that pressure was put on William Conolly's son to not renew the Club's lease on Montpelier. When it came up for renewal, he refused and ordered the Hell Fire Club from his property. Some say that in retaliation, the Club set fire to the House, and this is actually the origin of the great fire that all but destroyed Montpelier in the mid-1700s. Others say that the club simply set fire to the building during their drunken revels in order to give the place a more hellish appearance (if this is the case, it certainly worked!).

Another story maintains that a servant in the house accidentally spilled some whiskey on a new frock coat, which Burn the Chapel Whaley was wearing, ruining the material. In a fit of anger, the principle emptied the remainder of the bottle over the unfortunate man and set him ablaze. As the blazing man ran screaming down the stairs, he clutched at a tapestry hanging by the hall door. Within moments, the fire had spread, engulfing all in its path. Some members of the club were so drunk that they couldn't escape, but Whaley and some of his more sober companions managed to reach safety by leaping from the windows of the upper stories. Down in the city, the people watched the flames consume the building, rising against the night sky. The club relocated to a Stewards House at Killakee, several miles away, but it never enjoyed the same membership, and not long after, it broke up.

However, it was not completely the end of the Hell Fire Club. In 1771, it flourished again under a new name and with a new membership. Again, it used Montpelier House—now still mostly a burned-out ruin but with some serviceable areas—for some of its more ghastly ceremonies. It now called itself "The Holy Fathers" (or sometimes "The UnHoly Fathers" and its principal member seems to have been Thomas Whaley, widely known as "Buck Whaley," son of Richard Chappell Whaley, a prominent Dublin politician and a man hated and despised every bit as much as his father had been. And there was a subtle change in the ethos of the group—whereas the original Club had been (in theory at least) devoted to the furtherance of the darker mystic arts, the new grouping made no pretence at mysticism or magic, but was simply involved in orgiastic debauchery. As with the Hell Fire Club, stories cropped up about both the Club and Montpelier House. One claims that they kidnapped, raped, murdered, and ate a local farmer's daughter and that they practiced bestiality on a regular basis with local livestock. Some were said to be "vampires" drinking human blood on a regular basis within the confines of the house. It is said that Whaley eventually confessed his awful deeds and sought absolution from a Dublin clergyman before dying in 1800. After that the last incarnation of the Hell Fire Club passed away as well.

With such utter debauchery, vile behavior, and perhaps spilled human blood within its walls, many people believed that the very walls of the building had absorbed some of the evil that went on there. Many people who visited the place, which was now little more than a ruin (as evidenced by the report of the antiquarian Austin Cooper in 1779) experienced a "very uneasy feeling" within its precincts. Although the United Irishmen general Joseph Holt spent a night within its walls during the Rebellion of 1798 and experienced very little, several of the volunteers of Robert Emmet's followers also stayed there prior to a planned attack on Dublin in 1803 and were "greatly unsettled by the atmosphere within."

In 1800, the Conolly family sold Montpelier to Luke White, a prominent Dublin bookseller and politician. He had some grandiose plans for rebuilding the house, all of which came to nothing, and he was later forced to sell to the Massy family of Duntrileague, County Limerick (the Barons Massy), who also owned lands around Killakee. The family became bankrupt in 1924 with Hamon Massy, the 8th Baron Massy (known as "the Penniless Peer" in Dublin), and the lands were bought by the Irish State. Today it's managed by Coillte, which is a division of the Irish Forestry Commission.

Do buildings actually absorb something of the evil or misery that had unfolded within their confines? It is easy to laugh at such beliefs, but today the ruins of the house stand aloof and forbidding on their bleak summit, and from time to time people have heard screams drifting down toward Dublin or have seen strange lights flickering among their tumbled stones. Those who have struggled up the steep hill have noted that even on the calmest days, a brisk wind whistles about the summit and chills walkers to the bone. And as twilight settled over the Hills there is an unmistakable feeling that this is not a place for sane and wholesome people to be. Is it something from the distant pagan past or some lingering vestige of the infamy that was once perpetrated there by the Hell Fire Club? Who can say?

Mortemer Abbey

Normandy, France

"A place of lost souls…the abode, so they say,
of the wand'ring dead
What sad spectres walk its cloistr'd halls?"
—Thomas Rowley, *The Abbey at Sunset*

Like ancient castles, great and abandoned abbeys often hold a mesmerizing and fearful attraction for us. Perhaps it is the confined nature of such places: the gloomy corridors, the encompassing silence, and the patches of darkness under shadowy archways that is so suggestive to us. Maybe it is the brooding sanctity of such places, the memories of long-vanished religieux which haunts us as we view or visit them. There is sometimes something serenely calming about such sites, but there can be something terrifying, too.

The mysterious ruins of Mortemer, the first Cistercian Abbey in Normandy, are such a place. They lie deep in a wooded valley, part of the Forest of Lyons, roughly 34 kilometres southeast of Rouen in the District of Eure. Today, only remnants of the walls are standing, but they serve as a reminder of one of the most important abbeys in France and of what was one of the largest Cistercian abbeys in the world.

Mortemer was founded in 1134 by Henry I of England (1068–1135), son of William the Conqueror, as one of the earliest holy houses of the Cistercian Order in France. It was erected on a great area of marshland around the Fouillebroc River and a nearby lake, which was known in Latin as *mortuum mare,* literally "The Sea of the Dead" or "Dead Pond," which gave the abbey its name. The marshy region had pagan connotations, deemed to be the home of pre-Christian gods, and it was thought that the building of the holy house would take away these baleful associations and influences. During the 15th and early 16th centuries, the abbey was at the height of its powers, drawing much of its wealth from the nearby town of Rouen. It housed more than 200 monks and owned large swathes of land in the countryside, including farms, houses, hospices, and even a number of inns and public houses in some nearby villages. However with its increasing financial security, it had become lax in its ways and the abbots and monks had become more concerned with worldly things than their original vows of poverty, chastity, and seclusion. In fact, the abbey now operated more like a business than a place of piety.

According to legend, sometime during the 1500s, a local woman was brought to the abbey for examination by the monks. The woman was a *garrache,* a possessed person who had been overcome by the spirit of a wolf—in effect a female werewolf. She was chained in a room in the abbey whilst the monks tried to perform an exorcism upon her—an exorcism which, by all accounts, was only partially successful. If the unclean spirit had been driven from her, then it found shelter within the very stonework of Mortemer. Around 1884, so tradition states, a certain Roger Saboureau was poaching in the forest close to the Abbey ruins when he was certain that he was being spied upon. Turning around, he was confronted

by a large female wolf that looked as if it might attack him. Badly frightened, he fired his gun, killing the beast, and then fled deep into the woods. Later, he returned to find his own wife, lying in a pool of blood with a number of wounds on her body where he'd shot her. She had come into the woods to find him, but had she, too, been overcome by the spirit of the 16th-century wolf that still lurked amongst the tumbled stones of Mortemer Abbey? Was she too a garrache, one of the possessed? Many locals certainly thought so.

In the early 1600s, Mortemer's fortunes began to go into a slow decline due to a parliamentary dictate that non-ecclesiastical appointees would now manage the secular affairs of French holy houses. Like many others, the abbey had relied upon a steady stream of funds from their lands, and with that cut off, it gradually fell into decay. The numbers of Brothers there diminished, and by the French Revolution there were only about four or five of them living there, largely within the falling buildings. The Revolutionaries of course did not treat them kindly. They were falsely accused of a number of crimes against the state and were forced to hide in the wine cellars of the Abbey itself. There they were found and were executed without mercy, and it is said that their blood was mixed with wine from the broken casks and drunk by their murderers. Ever since then, the cellars of the place have had an excessively oppressive and claustrophobic atmosphere, and some people claim that they can still smell the stench of death there. Following the Revolution, the Abbey was sold to a wealthy local farmer, but changed hands a number of times and was recently in the hands of a certain Madam Charpentier, who created a museum there in 1985. All the same, the ghosts haven't gone away.

Secluded within the abbey is the Spring of St. Catherine, a natural fountain and well that is said to have strange powers. It was believed that if a young, un-married girl approached the spring on certain nights of the year and prayed hard and earnestly to God, she would see the face of her future husband looking back at her from the waters of the well. However, if the girl in question was less that virtuous or if she did not take the task seriously, something else would look back at her from the waters and she might find herself possessed. Many argued that it was better to stay away from the spring and have nothing to do with its magi-cal waters. "Better to die an old maid than to see the Devil," runs a local saying. There are also certain tales of a sinister guardian. One local old man told a tale of World War II when the area was under German occupation. A British parachutist from a crashed aircraft landed within the ruins of the monastery and in the vicin-ity of the spring. Lost in the dark of the ruin, he had no idea of the direction of a nearby farm where he hoped the French Resistance would be waiting. Something moved in the darkness, and out of the gloom came an eerie, cowled figure, dressed in long dark robes like a monk. It signalled to him as if to follow, and led him into the woods close by. Shortly after, they reached a farmhouse, a rendezvous of the Resistance, where he was welcomed and brought to safety. He told his hosts about the curious cowled figure who had guided him through the woods and they all fell silent and crossed themselves. Since the Revolution, there had been no monks at the Abbey. What the airman had seen was a ghostly guardian at St. Catherine's Spring.

Many visitors to the museum in recent times have experienced the sounds of heavy breathing close to the ancient cloister walls as if someone were standing very close at hand. Others have been aware of a threatening presence somewhere close.

"I thought that there was definitely somebody walking just behind me, matching me step for step," said Kenneth Kovacs, an American visitor to the site. "I could definitely hear the sounds of breathing and you get a feeling when there is somebody close to you. But when I turned around to see who it was, there was nothing, just a queerly shaped shadow where the sun had caught the cloister wall a bit awkwardly. It was all very eerie—but I felt a presence that was gone in a moment."

Toward the end of the 19th century, Mortemer passed into the ownership of the Delarue family. They were exceptionally wealthy Parisians and as soon as they acquired the abbey they left their home in the city and moved into it. They had hardly settled in when strange and disturbing things began to happen. At night, their children were terrified by unexplained noises and things moving in their bedrooms of their own accord. Much of this activity occurred in a part of the abbey known as the Pink Room and in the library next door to it. The lady of the house was convinced that a strange presence followed her along the passages, even on the brightest day, whispering in her left ear from time to time in a low and husky voice. She could not be sure, but she thought that the language might be Latin. Singing or chanting was heard far away across the abbey, but there was no explanation as to where the sound was coming from. Ghostly footsteps were everywhere, and doors opened and closed on a regular basis without anyone there. Mirrors and pictures fell from the walls during the night, and in the morning they were found face down on the floor. Incredibly, their glass was never broken. Although they were exploring some of the more remote areas of the Abbey, the family found a dreadful-looking wooden statute of a priest performing an exorcism in one of the rooms, and every one of them felt that this was somehow connected to the supernatural phenomena. The statue seemed to have a "knowing" feel to it, almost as if it was watching them for some malign purpose. Mr. Delarue noted with a shudder that the fingers on one hand of the wooden priest somehow seemed impossibly long.

Most mysteriously, cars belonging to the family that had been parked in a shed or in a backyard were covered in a strange, fine white dust. Mr. Delarue approached a local priest and had the place exorcised in 1921, but it seemed to have had little effect and his family sold up and moved away soon after.

The ghost that is perhaps most associated with Mortemer is the "White Lady," said by many to be the spirit of the daughter of the Abbey's founder. Matilda, daughter of Henry I, was born in 1102, and at the age of 12, was already married to the German Emperor Henry V. Later, she was married to Geoffrey Plantagenet, Duke of Anjou with whom she had a son, also called Henry, who would form the basis for the English Plantagenet royal line (King Henry II of England). However, her rebellious nature and certain scandals associated with her had led to a rift between her and her father, which led to Henry I more or less imprisoning her at Mortemer. Her sad, pale spirit is said to drift through the ruins of the abbey at certain times and many people have seen it. When seen, particular attention should be paid to the phantom's clothing. If the White Lady is wearing white gloves it is a good omen signalling prosperity, love, marriage, or perhaps even a birth within the family, but if she is wearing black, it signals death within the year.

The ruins are the site of some ferocious poltergeist activity. Lights and noises have been seen and heard throughout the abandoned abbey on many nights. Some of the sounds resemble human cries, others loud bangs and rumbles. Fallen stones are moved, and interior doors swing without reason.

"Sometimes people hear voices shouting as if somebody was in great pain," observed an old man of the district, as he stood on the path around the ruin. "Other times they hear a roaring, like an animal. Sometimes it's just noise—like things falling or being pushed about. But very loud!" He paused significantly. "All sorts of things move around in those ruins after dark."

It is not for nothing that these ancient ruins have acquired the title of "the most haunted site in France." Lying just beneath the calm tranquillity of Mortemer Abbey, lies another dark reality that stretches its tentacles out into our everyday world to touch the living as they pass. Even in the grounds of such a holy house, one can still feel that the touch is that of the dead!

The Old Abbey

County Limerick, Ireland

"'Wheesht, wheesht *acushla!'* says the old grandmother from her seat by the low fire, moving her pipe in her toothless mouth. 'There'll be no more talk o' ghosts an' witchcraft, for such things have no place in God's holy order. They're set against all the bishops and angels indeed.'"
—Mrs. Mallory, *The Rambling House*

By any standards, the ruins of St. Katherine's Augustinian Convent, Manis-terngalliaghduff—locally known as "the Old Abbey"—are an eerie place. Situated in a low valley about 2 miles from the village of Shanagolden, County Limerick, the ruins are overgrown with brambles and low trees, and access to them can be rather restricted. Yet, the very stones seem to ooze a kind of evil that is almost palpable even on the brightest day. The depression in which the ruin stands is surrounded by fields in where cattle often graze, and yet it is noticeable that no cattle venture close to the grey stone outer walls of the former convent. Nor do many birds nest in the nearby trees. Perhaps this is understandable seeing that such a place was allegedly closed on the orders of a pope because of its wickedness.

The convent was founded around 1298. The exact meaning of the name of the site on which it is situated has been open to argument—some have suggested that it means "the monastery of the black fair" signalling that there may have been some sort of dubious gathering on the location before the monastery was built. It may even have been a place of ritualistic pagan worship. At some time, it was thought that a Christian hermitage may have been erected on the site—perhaps to take away its pagan influences—from which the later monastery developed, described in records as St. Katherine's Ui Conaill, a place for the worship of Augustinian nuns. It is first mentioned in the early 1300s during an Inquisition (investigation by a Council) into the property of Thomas de Clare, a local landowner. It believed that it was entitled to a share of the rents, which de Clare was levying on a church in the region; the Abbey also claimed an interest in this as well. However, for at least part of its life, the Old Abbey seems to have been a tranquil and relatively holy place.

It is toward the end of its existence that the story becomes confusing and various strands of folklore connected to it start to appear. For instance, it's not exactly clear when the monastery was dissolved—some say that it was 1541, others that it was a hundred years later around 1642 during the Irish Rebellion. It is quite probable that it may have been closed around the time of the General Dissolution of the Monasteries (1536–1541) under the English King Henry VIII. However, a number of Irish religious houses stayed open long after the Dissolution (Bonnamargy Friary in North Antrim, for instance, was still conducting services, albeit in a limited capacity, as late as around 1650), so it's possible that St. Katherine's may have been in existence in the mid-1600s. What is known is that by 1700, it was abandoned.

No one is exactly sure how it closed, but a popular theory is that it was dissolved on the express orders of a pope—one of the very few in the world to be so dissolved. It is unclear who the pope was at the time, but given the suggested dates, two rather distinctive pontiffs could be identified. If the convent was closed in 1541, then the pope concerned would have been Paul III (1534–1549) a rather powerful pontiff and the first real leader of the Counter-Reformation. As such, he was a man determined to strengthen the authority of the Catholic Church across Europe in the face of Protestant advances. If St. Katherine's was closed in 1641, as some have suggested, then the pope in question would have been Urban VIII (1623–1644), a domineering pontiff with an avowed fear and detestation of witchcraft, which is significant as far as the affairs of St. Katherine's are concerned, as we shall see. First, however, we will examine another ghost, which is alleged to haunt the site, for the Old Abbey was reputedly already troubled at the time of its closure.

Here again the story is rather confusing. During the 1500s, large parts of Ireland were troubled by inter-clan wars in which the English were often involved. One of the great Gaelic houses—the Fitzgeralds, who were the Earls of Desmond and who held lands around Shanagolden establishing a castle there (Shanid Castle)—was almost perpetually engaged in warfare against other English-backed clans. Sometime during the mid-1500s, the wife of one of the Earls of Desmond was wounded in an attack on the castle and was taken to St. Katherine's to see if anything could be done for her by the nuns there. It was there she supposedly died and her grieving husband placed her in a stone tomb beneath the High Altar. Shortly afterward, the convent was attacked, the attackers believing that the Earl had taken refuge there, and the Earl and the nuns were forced to flee. When they were gone, the lady—who had only been in a stupor—came to and found herself entombed. She couldn't move the heavy stone slab above her and her screams rang through the now-abandoned Abbey until she was suffocated. Her ghost is now supposed to haunt the ruin, a shadowy shape that drifts between the stones, and sometimes her screams can still be heard, drifting over the nearby fields. It is said in some quarters that those who hear it will be dead within the space of a year.

The most prevalent story about St. Katherine's, however, is that it was once "a nest of witches." At some time in either the 16th or 17th century, a certain abbess took over. In their pamphlet *The History and Antiquities of St. Catherine's Old Abbey, County Limerick* (1903–4) the archaeologists J. Wardell and T. Westropp simply describe her as "a woman of the Fitzgeralds." Locally she is known as the Black Abbess or the Black Hag because she "infected" St. Katherine's with the scourge of witchcraft, corrupting many of the nuns there. The nature of the witchcraft is unknown, but it is whispered that it included raising the Devil and infant sacrifice, although it's more probable that the nuns simply dealt in potions and philtres. However, there were rumors that the pagan practices of former times were also carried on at the convent.

There have been rumors of Dark Magic in certain other Irish religious foundations. In the mid-1600s, the Dominican friary at Lough Urlaur (about three

miles from Kilkelly, County Mayo) was "possessed" by demons and several of the monks summoned up the Devil in the form of a huge black pig. This was eventually charmed out of the friary by an old piper (the Abbot had a dream in which an angel informed him that one good pipe tune, expertly played, was worth the prayers of a hundred bishops) and the holy house was restored. Nothing like that happened at Shanagolden. Indeed, the situation under the Black Abbess grew steadily worse and word of what was going on in Robertstown Parish (in which St. Katherine's stood) got back to the Primate of Ireland who referred the matter directly to Rome. The pope became involved and after reviewing the alarming tales of what appeared to be going on, simply ordered St. Katherine's to be closed, and the nuns there dispersed to other convents. This was done in either 1541 or 1641, depending on which source is believed.

The nuns were scattered across Ireland and disappeared—except for one. The Black Abbess continued to remain as a kind of recluse within the abandoned convent. How long she lived there is unknown, but it is thought that she continued to do so as the building decayed and fell around her. Today, the chancel of the old abbey is still known as The Black Hag's Cell. And, according to legend, she still continued to function as a black magician, preparing potions and love spells for those in the surrounding countryside. According to Westropp and Wardell, who received their account from the oral tradition, she was often seen late in the evening gathering herbs and growths along the laneways and in the woodlands. She was regarded with a great deal of fear by locals who made their way to the ruined abbey in order to buy her potions. She was also widely known throughout the district as a "cup tosser." This was a kind of prophetess and a forerunner of the person who could read tea leaves. It was probably predicting the future from the dregs of wine in a cup. The Abbess was believed to be so accurate in her prophesies that it was said that no noble in the area would make war on his neighbor without consulting with her first. But such prophesizing reeked of witchcraft and the evil of the Abbess's ways actually seeped into the very stones of the building, or so it's said.

The Abbess was found dead one morning amid the ruins of St. Katherine's convent by a passing pedlar. According to some accounts there had been a heavy frost and perhaps she had perished from hypothermia. Others say, however, that the Devil had come for her. Although she was dead, however, her evil spirit was not done with the ruin in which she had lived. Her likeness, dressed in black and with a black veil across her face, still drifts among the tumbled stones and through the twisted thicket around them. From to time, the specter will venture to the edge of the fields around the Old Abbey and look out across the countryside. It is said that all cattle which it "overlooks" will suffer some sort of illness—one good reason for keeping livestock from straying too close to the ancient walls.

And there's one other mystery connected with the old place. Hidden away somewhere within the ruin is a book so blasphemous that if a person were to read it without some form of holy protection, they would go mad. This is the Black Abbess's spell book and a record of the pagan rituals that were supposedly carried out on the site where the abbey now stands. Its covers are said to be of iron—perhaps to restrict the force of the spells within it, and this is sometimes given as another reason why animals (who are sensitive to such things) will not venture too close. It's said that there have been several attempts to find the book—if someone were to find it and be able to read it, they might acquire great power—but so far it hasn't been found. But even though its lies are hidden somewhere, its influence still may be felt in the cold chills of the ruin.

Of course, there are those who say that these things never happened—that the stories of witchcraft, pagan worship, and evil nuns lie merely in the imaginations of Protestant Reformers seeking to discredit the Catholic faith in the area. The tale is no more than ancient propaganda, they claim. But even they have to admit that the Old Abbey is an eerie place, a patchwork of crumbling walls and doorways that appear to lead nowhere. And when the sunlight starts to fade, a faint wind blows up and cattle start to move away across the nearby fields, shadows begin to move of their own accord between the trees. Is the tale of the Black Abbess truth or fiction? In the eerie twilight, one can't help but wonder.

Old Emmanuel Hill Church

Stull, Kansas

"Abandon all hope, ye who enter here."
—Dante Aligheri, *The Divine Comedy*

What would make a pope divert his flight plan? To avoid some place where Hell spills out onto earth? Or something incredibly evil smack in the middle of America? Could it be that one of the Seven Gateways to Hell in the world (see Houska Castle) lies somewhere in Kansas? Some people (including maybe even the late Pope John Paul II) seem to think so.

Between the towns of Lawrence and Topeka just off of Route 40, lies the tiny hamlet of Stull. As places go, there's not much to see in the village— a few houses, a store, and a couple of churches—and yet Stull has achieved something of a reputation for itself and continues to draw what the locals describe as "unwelcome visitors" throughout the year. It has appeared on a number of Websites and videos, and in 1992, a heavy metal band—Urge Overkill—released a CD entitled *Stull* with a picture of the settlement's old and abandoned Emmanuel Hill Church on the cover.

It is the cemetery of the church that has gained the place its sinister reputation, and which has been named as one of the "most evil spots in America." Indeed, it has been given as the location of one of the Gateways to Hell, which exist in the modern world, a suggestion which has carried the fame of this tiny hamlet far beyond the borders of rural Kansas. Each year, at times such as Halloween, droves of sightseers descend on Stull, much to the anger of local residents who claim that those who visit the cemetery at Emmanuel Hill are desecrating the graves of their loved ones. There are often rumors that Black Magic ceremonies are being carried on there by Satanists intending to raise the Devil. In fact, the situation has become so bad that the Douglas County Sheriff's Office now patrols the immediate area and its officers have the power to issue $100 fines for trespassing to those interlopers that they find within the cemetery boundaries. They also have the power to escort such people out of the hamlet. There is also the idea that the name of the hamlet derives from the word *skull,* referring to the skull of a demon (or a witch), which was found close to the Emmanuel Hill site. And, despite the measures of the local authorities, interest and discussion concerning the place (particularly on the Internet) still remains high. Stull, it seems, has formidable associations and a sinister past. Or does it?

Although the stories concerning the hamlet are legend—many of them involving diabolical revels and actual appearances by Satan himself—there seems to be no real history to them, for the notion of Hell's gateway is a surprisingly modern one. The hamlet originally started out as a settlement known as Deer Creek around the mid-1800s. It was a large farming community made up of solid, hard-working German, Dutch, and east European immigrants who were deeply religious and kept pretty much to themselves. Although relatively small, Deer Creek was large enough to have its own post office, as it lay on a postal route to Topeka. The postmaster there was Silvester (Sylvester) Stull, whose nationality is variously given as either German or Polish, and whose date of birth is given as March 19, 1862. He was the son of one of the settlement's founders, Isaac Stull, who had been regarded as something of a village patriarch and wise man. Given such an influential background, it was only natural that Silvester should rise to the position of postmaster for the relatively important Topeka route. He married in Deer Creek, his wife being Bertha Koehler, who bore him 11 children, all of whom were raised on the very edge of Emmanuel Hill cemetery. At the time, the old church was a thriving place, and all of Silvester and Bertha's children were baptised there. On retirement, however, Silvester and his wife didn't stay in Deer Creek, or even in Kansas, but moved to Orange County in California where he died on July 4th, 1931. However, the tiny community back at Deer Creek wished to record his contribution to the area and in 1899; they renamed their village after him. The Stull post office was closed in 1903 and so the hamlet name actually reflects the work of a local postmaster rather than the discovery of a diabolic skull, as has been claimed.

Stull did, however, have a number of factors that would later contribute to its sinister reputation. In 1970, the Emmanuel Hill Church was an eerie ruin sited above the hamlet and it did share the same postal zip code as Topeka— 666, said to be the number of the Devil. Moreover, in an old map of the area published in 1905, the principal route through the village is described as Devil's Lane. Marked on the same map is another feature described as The Devil's House. This was an abandoned two-story stone farmhouse located at the junction of 93rd Street and Paulin Road which survived into relatively recent times. The house had been abandoned for decades, and there were stories in the area that it was badly haunted. The boarded and inaccessible upper story was said to be frequented by demons. One investigator claimed that the downstairs of the building was used for Black Magic practices and that he had seen burnt black candles and inverted crucifixes there—all alleged signs of coven activity. The reputation of the Devil's House therefore may well have impacted on Stull.

Nearby Lawrence had its own particularly bloody history. In the early years of the Civil War, it was a base for pro-Union guerrilla bands such as the Kansas Red Legs and the Jayhawkers under Captain James H. Lane who raided deep into Missouri. At 5 a.m. on August 21st, 1863, a group of Confederate partisan raiders under the command of William Clarke Quantrill entered the town to take reprisal for an alleged Union attack on Osceola, Missouri, in September 1861. It was Quantrill's declared intention to "take Jim Lane's heart back to Missouri" (Lane had to escape by running through cornfields in his nightshirt). Quantrill then gave the order to "kill every man and burn every house" and whilst his men were doing this— and slaughtering women and children as well—the Confederate officer enjoyed breakfast. The killing was horrific, and more than 120 houses were

found to have been burned, many with the charred remains of occupants inside. The legacy of this terrible massacre left a blight on the entire region and may have left its mark on Stull, even though it did not feature in the killing.

The stories concerning the hamlet really took flight around the early 1970s, at a time when America was gripped by what might be called "Devil fever." In 1971, William Peter Blatty released his famous novel *The Exorcist,* a classic tale about demonic possession, which by 1973, had become a blockbuster screen adaptation that shocked the entire country and spawned countless imitations. Among such films were *The Omen* and Michael Winner's *The Sentinel,* which centered around a gateway to Hell in the middle of a busy city. These quickly became a significant part of American culture at the time, and as in medieval days, people became obsessed with the idea of demons and the Devil.

All this "diabolism" seemed to more or less pass Stull by. There were, of course, some old ghost and witch stories about the place, but probably no more than in any other small community. One of these tales that surfaced in the mid-1960s concerned a large tree that grew in the middle of the cemetery of old Emmanuel Hill Church. The church was something of a falling ruin, having been abandoned in 1922 when its congregation outgrew its confines and moved to a more modern place of worship. This particular tree—a massive spreading pine—had somehow managed to encompass one of the nearby gravestones in the churchyard so completely that the funeral marker seemed to have become a part of the growth itself. The stone marked the final resting place of Bettie and Frankie Thomas, both of whom had died in 1879. Somehow, an unfounded rumor began to circulate that these two had been witches and were involved in Satanic rites in the churchyard. It was further said that both of them had been killed together by witch-hunters from Kansas. Of course, there was no real basis for such stories, although older people in Topeka didn't seem so sure—the community at Deer Creek had been a tightly-knit and rather reclusive one. So a number of old tales were resurrected around the Kansas firesides. As late as 1969, stories were circulating among local teenagers that Emmanuel Hill Church had been burned by Satanists and that its grounds were still used for their rites. Nothing could have been further from the truth, of course, but these stories were destined to have a profound influence later.

In 1974, an article appeared in the University of Kansas student newspaper, *The University Daily Kansan,* concerning Stull and carrying the headline "Legend of Devil Haunts Tiny Town." It leaned heavily on the demon-obsessed mood created by *The Exorcist* and claimed to have been based on regional stories and widely accepted local mythology. He claimed the recollections of elderly people in the settlement and the experiences of those who had visited Emmanuel Hill Churchyard and confronted supernatural beings. It was, said the article, only one of two places on earth where Satan appeared in his full majestic form. The article went on to state that such knowledge was "well known" in the hamlet, but that local people "kept it to themselves." A student from Bonner Springs subsequently wrote that her grandmother had told a tale about "a mayor of Stull" (Stull has never really had a formal mayor—in 1857, the settlement only consisted of six families) who did a deal with the Devil in return for personal favors, allowing him to appear on certain nights of the year within the limits of Emmanuel Hill Church. This tale lead back to an actual incident that occurred in Deer Creek, about 1850. According to tradition, a leading citizen of the village was murdered by a stablehand who was then hanged without trial by the dead man's kinfolk at the scene of his crime. The awful and bloody murder was said to have been conducted in a barn on the site of which Emmanuel Hill was later built. There was also the tale of a suspected witch buried within the cemetery precincts whose descendants still live in the Stull area as werewolves.

Such tales were extremely fanciful, but by 1980, they were starting to appear in a wider press. *The Kansas City Times* began to publish articles about the cemetery, full of dubious detail—for instance, one of the headstones bore the name "Witch" (which appears to have been a surname, but it was said that the Devil visited this particular grave on certain occasions); that there had been Black Masses going on in the church since 1850 (this ignored the fact that Emmanuel Hill had not been built until 1867 and the burying ground had not been laid out until 1869); that it was founded by immigrants from a town in England that bore the same name and which had suffered a number of witch persecutions, or that it had been settled by sorcerers fleeing the Salem Witch Trials in Massachusetts in 1692.

The most persistent legend, however, is of a flight of worn steps that lead from the church down into the darkness. These will lead those who dare to venture down them directly to Hell. It is said that these steps may exist, but that they lead to an underground vault, which was allegedly used for burials. However, the location of these steps varies with each tale. Some accounts say that they lie to the right of the ruined building; others say they are behind it; other still say that they lie behind the retaining walls of some of the family plots. One of the plots is identified as that of Geneva Stull (a descendant of Silvester?) who died in 1920. It is said that if one even goes part of the way down these steps, time will pass at a different rate, and though it seems as if only a few minutes have passed, centuries will actually have gone by. There is no evidence that these steps actually exist, but this has not stopped thrill-seekers looking for them and the accompanying gateway to Hell. In language reminiscent of the film *The Sentinel*, many warn of dire consequences to those who investigate.

On March 20, 1978, a crowd of almost 150 people (mainly University of Kansas students) gathered in Stull cemetery to see if the Devil would appear. Legend hinted that those who had died violent deaths would rise up to meet him and at midnight would dance in the graveyard with Satan. However, the only spirits that appeared in the cemetery came from a bottle. But the stories continued unchecked and by 1989 the crowds in the cemetery on Halloween night had grown so large that the Douglas County Sheriff's Office had to station special deputies around the site to discourage ghost-hunters and to charge those who were caught in the area with trespass. Graffiti, beer cans, and fast food containers were now littering the site, and the mood of locals changed from mild bemusement into downright anger as they saw their community being vandalized. And although stories continue to be printed in newspapers and magazines, local people insisted there is nothing in them. There is no gateway to Hell in Stull. Or is there?

In 1993, as part of an American Papal visit, Pope John Paul II flew to Colorado in order to conduct a Mass there. It is reported (in no less a publication than *Time* magazine) that the pontiff specifically requested that his plane take a detour around Kansas into Nebraska and then to Colorado. His flight path would have taken him over eastern Kansas, right over where Stull is located, and it was rumoured that the Holy Father did not wish to fly over an opening leading directly to Hell itself. This may just be a rumor, but maybe the pope knew something that the rest of us do not!

There is now not much to see in Stull. According to a local Lawrence newspaper, Emmanuel Hill Church was mysteriously torn down on the night of March 29th, 2002, and all that remains is a pile of rubble. No one knows who demolished the building— according to the local landowner, a Major Weiss, he gave no instructions for the church to be pulled down, and no one has owned up to it. Yet another mystery. And what of the gateway to Hell? Is it still there? Does anyone want to go and find out?

Salimgarh Fortress

Delhi, India

"There are Officers Quarters in Mian Mir whose doors open without reason and whose furniture is guaranteed to creak, not with the heat of June, but with the weight of the Invisibles who come to lounge in the chair...."
—Rudyard Kipling, "My Own True Ghost Story" from *The Phantom Rickshaw*

India is a land of legend and mystery. Here, the lore and traditions of ancient days seem to blend seamlessly with the modern world. Ghosts are as much a feature of Indian life as they are in the West—perhaps more so. The phantoms of women who have died in childbirth, old men who have died from starvation, and children who have perished in appalling circumstances seem to appear with a kind of regularity, begging for alms or pricking at the consciences of the more well-off. Arguably more than any other country in the world, in India the idea of the supernatural is more closely linked with a sense of justice and equanimity.

It is perhaps this sense of unequal justice that underpins many of the ghosts that haunt the ancient fortress of Salimgarh on the Yamuna River, which flows through Delhi—probably India's most haunted stronghold. Far older than the neighboring Red Fort, Salimgarh has been renamed Swatantrata Senani Smarak (Freedom Fighters Memorial) and is now a museum. Even so, it still retains much of its ancient atmosphere and mystery. The lore attached to the site and the feelings that many visitors have experienced there are rooted in the building's turbulent history.

The fortress was built on an island in the Yamuna by Islam Shah Suri (1545–1554) also known as Jalal Khan, the second ruler of the brief Sur Dynasty, which reigned over that part of India for part of the 16th century, and which expanded the town of Delhi as its capital. The Sur rulers were Islamic Pathans from Bihar who briefly overthrew the Mughal Emperors who had initially ruled Afghanistan, Pakistan, and parts of Northern India. The second Mughal Emperor, Humayan, had started building up Delhi, but found himself under attack from the Sur rulers and was driven out of the town. Islam Shah Suri then built a fortress on the river to protect his newly acquired capital. The name *Salimgarh* simply means Salim's Fort, and the place was considered to be impregnable and well able to stand against the Mughals. Although a largely ineffectual ruler, Humayan was determined to take back the town and launched a ferocious assault against it in 1555. During the various battles, many prisoners were captured and were taken back to Salimgarh to be tortured and executed. Their wails and groans can still be heard today by visitors to the site. By this time, the Sur Dynasty was in upheaval; Islam Shah Suri was already dead, his 12-year-old son was assassinated by a rival faction, and the fortress fell again to the advancing Mughal forces. It was to become an army camp for the various Mughal Emperors.

During the reign of the powerful Mughal ruler Aurangzeb I (1666–1707), the so-called "Conqueror of the World," Salimgarh was once again converted into a prison and a house of torture. Although a strong monarch, Aurangzeb was a despot and many of those who rose against him were condemned to languish within its sombre walls were they were subjected to horrific deprivations and abuse. It was said that Aurangzeb instructed his warders to wash the stone walls with the blood of those whom they had beaten and maltreated as a warning to all others who would rebel against him. Thus, the misery of the prisoners was actually ingrained into the very stones of the place and added to the chilling atmosphere.

The most frequently seen ghost within the fortress's precincts is that of a shrouded lady who wanders across the battlements and is seen in the courtyard as well. Sightings of her state that she is always wrapped in white with glittering jewelry. According to local tradition, this specter is that of Zebunissa, Aurangzeb's eldest daughter. She was said to be his favorite child (her name means "Ornament of the Throne"), a woman who was very gentle and a popular and accomplished poetess. In fact, 50 years after her death in 1707, her major diwan (a collection of poems) was discovered and circulated; it was said to be the most beautiful verse anywhere in India. Deeply religious, she was interested in Sufism (a mystical form of Islam) and much of her writing reflects this. She also gave up wearing grand Islamic black clothes, signifying importance at the Mughul Court, and took to wearing simple white garments, becoming known as Zaib-al-Tafari (Worthy of Praise) for her humility and devotion. However, the times in which she lived were greatly unsettled within the Mughal Empire and her despotic father had many enemies who wished to see him overthrown. One of those who conspired against him was Zebunissa's brother Akbar to whom she was very much attached. Perhaps very unwisely, she wrote him several letters of support abhorring their father's tyranny all across the Empire. When, in 1681, a number of elements elected Akbar as Emperor, Aurangzeb moved quickly and viciously to reestablish his authority and put down the rebellion. In the course of his reprisals, he found the letters that Zebunissa had written to her brother. Although he had killed many of those who had stood against him or had been complicit in the rising, Aurangzab could not bring himself to slay his daughter. Instead, he had her imprisoned in Salimgarh from where she wrote to him many times, begging for her release. Each time her request was turned down, and, hearing of her father's death in 1707, Zebunissa herself passed away. However, her ghost remained to haunt her prison. According to some accounts, the phantom appears on the ramparts of the Fortress singing some of her own couplets and enchanting all who hear them.

Somehow, however, certain accounts of her phantom appear to have been confused with some other dark Indian entity. When she lifts her veil, it is said, she reveals not the beautiful face of the Zaib-al-Tafari, but that of a hideous green-skinned creature with sharp and vicious-looking teeth. This may be the face of a rakshasa or a churel, both forms of Indian vampires (the latter being the demonic spirit of a woman who has died in childbirth—a common type of ghoul in Far Eastern lore). Such a countenance signals the doom of the viewer as the thing may well attack. The lady in white is to be avoided at all costs!

By the 1850s, the British were well established in India, and in 1857, the powers and substantial lands of the British East India Company were transferred to the British Monarchy, in the person of Queen Victoria, ushering in a period of British Colonial Rule known as the British Raj. 1857 was also the date of a major mutiny of Indian troops often referred to as the Sepoy Rebellion or the Indian Mutiny. The causes for the Mutiny are very complex and had partly to do with relations between the East India Company and local taluqdars (rural landlords) who felt that Company agents were unnecessarily meddling in their affairs without fully understanding them, particularly the Caste system. The tipping point, however, was the use of cartridges for the new Enfield 1853 Pattern Rifle, which was used by the Company Army and contained many Indian Muslim troops or sepoys. The rifle barrels had a tighter fit and the gunpowder came in paper cartridges, the ends of which had to be bitten off to release it during reloading. These cartridges were coated in grease made from pig fat to protect them from dampness. Of course, no Muslim would bite into pork fat, as it would be offensive to their religion, and if the British authorities were to use beef fat, this would be offensive to Hindu sepoy brigades (because the cow was a sacred animal in the Hindu religion). Nevertheless, the British went ahead and issued some of the cartridges and, although they were subsequently withdrawn, rumors persisted among the native soldiers that new cartridges were secretly greased in both pork and beef fat. The situation came to a head in the Bengal Native Infantry, a branch of the Bengal Army in which there were already problems. The Mutiny spread across the Indian sub-continent and the British were forced to act. Using Salimgrah as a holding and interrogation center, they shipped Mutineers there for "questioning" which, it is believed, often involved physical abuse. The sense of injustice against religious beliefs and practices was overwhelming.

By this time the Mughal Empire had been so driven back by the British that the current Emperor, Bahdur Shah Zafar II only ruled a small amount of land around Delhi. Even so, he was taken prisoner by the British—he was captured almost beside Humayan's tomb—and briefly held in Salimgar where he conspired with a number of the Mutineers. In retaliation, he was beaten and starved, and it is said that his emaciated and bloodied ghost still wanders some of the corridors of the old Fortress, even though he was later moved to Rangoon in Burma and was only there for a brief period. He was really the last of the Mughal rulers of the area and was certainly badly treated by the British during his brief stay. The sense of injustice follows his specter like a pall.

On July 8th, 1858, a peace treaty was signed between the British at the Mutineers in the town of Gwalior, south of Agra. Although the Rebellion was over, some prisoners were still held in Salimgarh, although the British Army used Lal Quila (Red Fort now in the Old Quarter of Delhi which had been completed in

1648) as their cantonment (headquarters for military forces/police) during most of the Raj. However, it's said that Salimgarh was used as an intelligence post for housing political prisoners and rebels who spoke out against British rule. There seems little doubt that, like the Mughal Emperors before them, the British used torture deep in some of the rooms of the Fortress in order to obtain their information.

The Fort remained in British hands until the end of their rule in India in 1945. For the latter part of the time (1940–47), it was a prison that held members of the Indian National Army. This was a Nationalist organization formed during World War II in order to bring an end, by terrorist means, to the British Raj, and to drive the British out of India with the aid of the Japanese. These men considered themselves to be Freedom Fighters, fighting the oppressive British regime, and it is in their memory that Salimgarh enjoys its modern name. Their ghosts are supposed to wail in the cells of the Fortress each night.

With such a violent and turbulent history, is it any wonder that the Fortress is frequented by ghosts? Many visitors and those working late within the walls claim to have heard and glimpsed things—distant voices, shouts, and even vicious laughter. Usually, however, when an attempt is made to find the source of these sounds, they die away altogether. And if anecdotal accounts are to be believed, many people have experienced what sounded like footsteps, which seemed to follow them, accompanied by a blast of cold air on their backs. Yet, when they turn round, there is no one there. As with other ancient sites, visitors have felt unaccountable catches on their arms or tugs at their sleeves, again with nobody there. The sense of foreboding and anguish is very strong within the walls of Salimgarh according to many people—perhaps the terrible pain of the tortured *has* actually found its way into the stones of the place.

A violent history, an imprisoned princess, and torture chambers from both the Mughal and British eras have all contributed to the ominous traditions of Salimgarh. Is it any wonder the place is creepy?

Spokeveld

Great Karoo, South Africa

"And sometimes in the campfire's burnished glow,
Flick'ring shadows come and go."
—John Anthony, *Along the Trail*

It's easy enough to imagine an old castle or a Gothic mansion as being haunted; such things are the stuff of stories and films—but what about an entire stretch of land? Can a "country" be haunted just as much as any house? Can ghosts throng just as much to open territory as they would to any structure? In South Africa, it seems they can.

On the edge of the Great Karoo in the Western Cape Province of South Africa lies an area known as Spokeveld (Ghost Field or Ghost Country in the Afrikaner language of the Cape). The Karoo is a hot and arid desert-like expanse that extends for more than 400,000 square miles into the Cape, and is one of the world's most unique arid zones. The word comes from an indigenous Khoisan word that means "dry thirst country" and refers to a land that is not altogether desert, but at the same time is not too far from it in nature.

The area around the Karoo was settled by a combination of Afrikaner Dutch, German, and British who built small settlements in the area, many of which have expanded and still survive. Towns of varying sizes such as Beaufort West (named for the 5th Duke of Beaufort, British Governor of the Cape Colony), Klaarstroom, and Gamkasloof (once counted as one of the world's most isolated settled communities) dot the arid landscape, their names hinting at the varied heritage of the region. Settlers arrived from Europe, venturing in to the seemingly inhospitable interior of the Cape and bringing their own ways and beliefs with them. Prior to the building of the first road through the region by Adam de Schmit between 1856 and 1858, they arrived in trains of covered wagons, very much like the early settlers of the American West. And like the American pioneers, they suffered great hardship and loss in the wastes of the Cape desert country—wagon trains were wiped out by disease, some suffered starvation, others simply disappeared. It was around these early explorations that many of the legends of the Karoo are based.

The area along the edges of the Great and Little Karoo have always been haunted, particularly the region that lies between the Patates River and the Southkloff. The Khoisan tribes of the area (the Khoisan comprise two ethnic groupings which are distinct from the Bantu people) claim that it is a place where the spirits of dead ancestors go to rest and hunt. The lights and smokes of their ghostly fires can be seen, it is claimed, for many miles around, and their eerie hunting cries can be heard in the darkness of the Cape night. And from time to time, groups of ghostly figures can be seen at a distance, walking through the scrub like hunters, only to melt away into the sunlight as soon as they are glimpsed. In fact, it may have been the Khoisan themselves who first referred to the area as a ghost country or ghost land.

This idea was quickly seized on by the settlers who arrived in the region. Many of them had their own ideas about ghosts that might not have been all that far removed from the Khosian notions, and soon these mingled with the native lore to characterize the area. The eerie cries in the dark, once attributed to ghostly hunting parties, now became the shouts of lost Afrikaner wagon trains seeking help in the wilderness. The mysterious and distant figures often glimpsed at twilight were not African ancestor spirits, but those of wandering settlers, lost amongst the scrub. Not only this, but ghostly settlements came and went, perhaps reflecting the tiny immigrant transitory villages that came and went in the harsh conditions. Small clusters of wooden houses and lone cabins have often been seen along the edges of the Great Karoo only to vanish as soon as someone approaches them. One of the most common stories is that of a small wooden one-roomed cabin that seems to regularly appear along the roadside several kilometers east of Beaufort-West. It has an old man sitting on its porch, sometimes smoking a long-stemmed German pipe of antique design, sometimes reading a newspaper and with a dog sleeping at his feet. If anyone approaches the house, it ripples and disappears like a reflection in a pool when the water is disturbed. The cabin also appears at night with a light burning in its single window as if to lure the visitor in. Some people say that those who enter are never seen again. There is no real tale for the origin of the cabin or of the old man, although some old tales say that there was indeed some form of dwelling there at one time, but that a family lived in it. A terrible fever wiped them all out as it passed through the area, but their ghostly cabin will appear from time to time, and whomever tried to enter it will contract the same fatal fever that killed them. From time to time, a small settlement of lean-to houses will appear in the scrub country. Such small places resemble the temporary shanty towns that were set up in the early 1800s by the Afrikaners who passed through the region. Indeed, travelers have seen women moving between the shanty houses, dressed in what might be referred to as "old fashioned clothing," the long skirts and dresses of former years. Like the lone cabins in the scrub, these too ripple and vanish like water if approached.

And there are individual ghosts that haunt the area, too. One of the most famous in the Karoo and in Beaufort-West is that of Elize Meiring, the Maid of Hex River. Her ghost is seen wandering in her nightgown, all the way along the River, between Beaufort-West and the splendidly named Hex (Witch) Mountains. This sprang from an old tale among the settlers that was widely told around the campfires and that may have had a European origin. Elize was known locally as the "heks" (heks is an Afrikaner name for a witch or person of disreputable background) of the Hex River. Elize lived with her parents who were honest farming people—the location of their homestead shifts with each telling of the tale— but she was very spoiled. She was also extremely beautiful, but didn't have the personality to match her looks. Even so, young men often came to pay court to her and, knowing how good-looking she was, she often set them near impossible tasks to prove how much they wanted her company. Her favorite "task" was to send a young man into the high Hex Mountains in order to bring back a rare red disa—a type of flower—that grew there. Only then would she consent to walk out with him. Many tried, but were turned back by the climb or by the terrible conditions on the upper slopes. One young man, however, did make it to the valley and picked a disa, but on the return journey, he missed his footing and fell to his death, still clutching the rare and precious flower. The tragic incident mentally unhinged Elize when it was relayed to her, and her parents were forced to lock her in her room to prevent her from doing herself any harm. One night, however, she managed to break out of the house and, still wearing her nightdress, fled either to the place where the young man had fallen or to the Hex River itself (depending on which version of the story is recounted). There she threw herself to her doom. Her anguished ghost, still clad in her nightgown, wanders the wilderness around the Hex River and the Great Karoo, laughing insanely and clutching a small red flower in her right hand, which she shows to anyone that she encounters.

In the seemingly endless scrub, there are frequent stories of ghostly camps out in the bush. Occasionally, strange and distant lights are seen, late at night, far out in uninhabited areas of the Karoo where no lights should be. These seem to signal the fires and lanterns of isolated camps, which seem to come and go in a mysterious way. A common tale in many parts of the Spokeveld is of a lone traveler stumbling into a small camp late at night where a fire is burning and a number of old men, dressed in the clothing of former years, are making a meal. The traveler is given some of their food, which is remarkably tasteless (among some of the African tribes, the food of ghosts is always bland and tasteless) before lying down to sleep. When he or she awakes, the camp is gone without trace and there is no sign of the fire, which was burning brightly the night before. In some cases, the old men around the fire have white and expressionless faces and disappear as soon as their fire is approached. The fire also vanishes without trace.

But many of the main stories concerning the region relate to the wagons in which the early settlers traversed the waste. Drivers along the Mieringspoort claim to have frequently seen distant wagons traveling across the uneven ground, even in daylight, only to vanish like smoke in the rays of the sun. Some have even encountered them.

Around the 1920s, a man named Major Ellis (an English settler) recounted in a journal what must be one of the most widely told tales of the region. He recounts it as a personal experience that happened many years earlier. Both he and an Afrikaner driver, Anthony de Beer, were traveling in an open wagon from Ceres to Beaufort-West late one evening. On a particularly uneven stretch of ground, the wheel came off their wagon and they stopped to fix it. As they worked, the light began to fail, and suddenly, away in the distance, both men heard the sound of another wagon approaching extremely fast. At first, Ellis thought that it was some sort of vehicle being driven recklessly along the road and that it would smash into them, but upon listening, de Beer said that he didn't think the sound came from the road at all. The wagon suddenly appeared, going at a fearful speed with the driver hunched forward over his horses. Ellis caught a glimpse of his face as the wagon shot past—it was skull-like and deadly white, with hard and glittering eyes, the lower portion covered in what looked like some sort of dirty bandana holding the jaws together. Looking up, de Beer shouted "Where the Devil are you going at such a speed?" The driver turned his head slightly and answered "To Hell!" Then with a peal of demonic laughter, the wagon passed and disappeared into the distance. A great waft of cold air chilled the men by the roadside. Ellis didn't know what to make of the whole incident, but Anthony de Beer was greatly depressed. He remembered an old Afrikaner legend about a phantom wagon, driven by the dead—those who saw it were doomed to die. However, if it was more than one who witnessed the phantom and one spoke to it (as de Beer had done), then the death fell upon the individual who spoke. By crying out to the specter, de Beer had doomed himself. One week later, Anthony de Beer's body was found, together with a crashed wagon at the bottom of a cliff. He appeared to have driven off the edge, even though he was an experienced wagoneer.

But it is not only minor demons and pioneer ghosts that haunt the edges of the Spokeveld. The region boasts some more modern phantoms, too. For instance, a young girl killed when falling from the back of a motorbike in the late 1960s is said to haunt the roads near Unionville. She solicits a lift, and as she gets into the vehicle the driver is always struck by the smell of apple blossom. However as the vehicle moves off, she fades away, although the smell lingers for a while. More recently a phantom, white-colored car has haunted the Port Elizabeth Highway between the Hex Mountains and the Drakensberg, driven wildly and apparently accounting for some of the accidents out there.

So, can an entire region be haunted? Can a whole area draw the spirits of the past to it from the realms beyond? As the light dims and the African night falls over the Spokeveld, you'd be inclined to think so!

Studley Park

New South Wales, Australia

"Lower still lay the Manor House—red brick with grey litchened mullions, a house in a thousand, Elizabethan—and from its twisted, beautiful chimneys, no smoke rose."
—Edith Nesbit, *The Haunted Inheritance*

Standing near the outskirts of Sydney, the weathered façade of Studley Park suggests a haunted house. Although it is the centerpiece for Camden Golf Club, it still has the reputation of being one of Australia's most haunted houses. The building certainly has a colorful and turbulent history, and one that leaves it open to the influences of the supernatural.

The house was built in 1889 by William Payne, who had bought land in an area called Narellan in southwest Sydney. He called his new property Studley Park, after another property of the same name which was believed to be near Ripon, Yorkshire, England. The house was also meant to impress his new wife, Claire Adams, who he had married in 1886. It was also meant to include four workers' cottages that would be built on the property and were designed to give it "a period feel." The house was designed by Francis Buckle, a prominent architect in Sydney, according to Payne's instructions and work began on the house by the builders A. L. & G. McCredie, early in 1889. Local people laughed at Payne, marvelling at the isolation and the expense of such a mansion, christening it "Payne's Folly." Although Payne paid no attention to their jibes, the house was to prove his undoing. Land had to be drained, timber of a specific kind had to be brought in, certain tiling and fittings had to be brought overland (and sometime overseas), and although this certainly was done, the expense of the place mounted. Soon it became too much for William Payne's wallet, and although the house was up and was a fine Victorian-looking mansion, he was almost bankrupt and still owed money. His principal creditor was Francis Buckle, the architect who had designed the place, and who was now threatening to take him to court. Payne was broken and had really no option but to sell Studley Park. However, there were no buyers, and under Australian law, Buckle was entitled to seize the property against payment of debt. This he did, leaving Payne shattered and destitute. Buckle used Studley Park as a weekend retreat for a time, but he was never happy there. Something mournful hung over the house—perhaps it had some sort of remembrance of its original owner, William Payne. It would not allow Buckle to settle, and in the end, he sold it on to a Dr. Henry Oliver in 1902. Oliver was the headmaster of the Camden Grammar School, which was located in St. Helen's Park House in nearby Campbelltown. His school had been expanding, and Oliver was seeking new premises that could serve as a new location for his seat of learning. Studley Park seemed to be just what he was looking for. Around the beginning of 1903, the new Camden Grammar School opened as a boarding school and continued to grow and develop throughout the subsequent years. However, local legend says that it remained a mournful place with a history of minor accidents and illnesses among staff and students there—perhaps a little more than similar institutions of the day.

The first real tragedy occurred on October 15th, 1909. A 14-year-old boarder named Ray Blackstone and five of his classmates decided to go swimming in a dam close to the school. It was a warm day (during winter in Australia temperatures are around 50 to 60 degrees F) and despite being warned about the dangers of swimming in the dam, the boys went anyway. Ray, who was a strong swimmer, tried to swim from one side of the dam to the other, but halfway over, ran into difficulties. In spite of the efforts of one of the other boys, Sydney Langford, he went under and drowned. His body was brought ashore by some of the senior boys and was reputedly laid out in the dark cellar of Studley Park to await transport home for burial.

Following the drowning, there were rumors of strange sounds and noises throughout the house, lights were allegedly inexplicably switched on and off, and wet footprints were found in some of the corridors. Ray Blackstone's figure was sometimes seen both inside and on the grounds of the house, disappearing as soon as anyone approached it. Furthermore, all the clocks in the house mysteriously moved to different times, often throwing the school day into confusion. The atmosphere of the old house became more oppressive. A number of the more sensitive students seemed less than happy there—maybe even frightened.

In 1919, the school was sold, 10 years after Ray Blackstone's death. The buyer this time was the Reverend Charles Herbert Palmer, who believed he could "make a go" of it as a Christian boy's school, but the heavy, sombre atmosphere of the old place often seemed to militate against this. In 1933, the school was packed up and moved to Manly, and to the house of William Bede Dalley, the Parliamentary Member for Sydney.

The house changed hands again. This time, he purchaser was Adolphus Gregory, who was a Senior Sales Manager with the Australian arm of Twentieth Century Fox, a man with a definite flair for the creative arts. He went to work on Studley Park, reshaping it and refurbishing in an art-deco style as befitted his temperament. The old students' dining hall was turned into a mini-theaterette and, as a keen golfer, Gregory converted the lawn into a nine-hole course, which was later extended to 18 holes. The stables at the back of the house (which had been used as classrooms in the time of the school) became a kind of golf club for the media mogul and his friends. Even though the companionship was good, many visitors claimed that they often felt uneasy around the place—there was a sort of "uncomfortable" feeling around the building, which actually alarmed some of them. Some claimed to have seen a young boy "dripping wet" in some parts of the course, but nobody could explain who he was. Could it have been the unsettled spirit of Ray Blackstone? All the descriptions coincided, although very few of the visitors actually knew of the earlier tragedy. Even Gregory often admitted to feeling uneasy when in the building. This feeling of apprehension was confirmed in 1939 when Gregory's son Noel died in the theaterette of advanced appendicitis. Gregory was devastated, and the paranormal activity around the house seemed to increase. Doors opened and closed of their own volition, voices were heard along the corridors, lights were found blazing after dark in rooms where there had been nobody present, electrical equipment only functioned intermittently for no reason, and strange and unidentified figures were seen "at a distance" in the grounds. In the end, Gregory could stand it no longer and moved away. He said the house "was far too creepy" and held too many difficult memories for him.

As World War II came to the Pacific, the property was taken over by the Australian Department of Defence and became the Eastern Command Training School for the training of the Armed Forces. Its accommodation was increased to house more than 280 staff attending the training courses there. One of the graduates from this facility was Lieutenant L.A. Cutler, who would go on to become a Governor of New South Wales. Nevertheless, even during the military occupation of the house, things were still not all that settled. Once again, electrical equipment only worked intermittently, odd voices were heard on field radios operating within the grounds, and strange footfalls were heard in rooms that were not being used at the time. Chairs were inexplicably pushed against cabinets and papers were strangely scattered around certain rooms. Many service personnel experienced the feeling that there was somebody walking behind them along some of the corridors, even when there was nobody there and personal possession, were moved—sometimes away across the house—for no reason.

But it was the cellar where Ray Blackstone's body had been allegedly laid out, which evoked the most discomfort. Some of the service personnel—some of them hard-bitten servicemen—simply would not venture down there, because they had the feeling that they were being watched from the shadows. The cellar was used as a sort of general storeroom for various bits and pieces—pieces of equipment, storage crates, and so forth—and therefore was in reasonably constant use. But few people liked going down there—it was "creepy," and there was always the sensation that somebody was "standing directly behind you." Some people even declared that they could hear breathing in the dark. Again, there seemed to be wet footprints all around.

And there was that same melancholy sensation about the house that other people had experienced before. Although it did not directly interfere with the training, the place didn't exactly make people feel happy and content, and many were glad when they graduated. At its peak, however, Studley Park could accommodate 250 trainees with an additional 250 under canvas in the main grounds of the house. Quite a lot of Army personnel to terrify!

In 1951, and with the War over, the Women's Royal Australian Army Corps took over Studley Park as a training base. However, the experience was not a happy one, and the stories of ghosts and mysterious happenings increased. Many of the recruits felt uneasy in the place, and once again, many clocks within the building inexplicably showed different times and warning bells went off without reason—frightening some of the women there. There were unexplained cold pockets and some women claimed they heard voices calling at odd hours of the night. Indeed, by the beginning of 1952, the Army was considering closing the site down and moving the WRAAC Training Centre to Mildura. Approval was rapidly given, and in June 1952, the Centre moved, leaving Studley Park to its ghosts and voices.

In 2001, however, the house became the site for an Australian television psychology reality show entitled *Scream Test.* In this, four contestants were locked in the old house for a night and had to record their fears and experiences to the camera. Mid-way through the night, one of the contestants refused to take part any further. He had heard voices, he claimed, and had distinctly heard a baby cry from the corner of one of the rooms. The experience had terrified him, and he was leaving the show. Some time after—and following another series of television investigations—Studley Park became the centerpiece of the Camden Golf Club course.

There is one final twist: In 2010, workmen were doing some repairs on behalf of the Club and were fixing up loose slates on the house's roof. As they worked they all experienced the same "creepy" feeling that others had talked about. They worked on, trying to make the 120 year-old roof watertight—then they made a chilling discovery. Under a slate, they found a hangman's rope tied in a noose attached to one of the beams. There was no explanation for this, but the "creepy" feeling grew much stronger. The rope was removed and the feeling passed. The story appeared in the *Camden Advertiser*, and the ghostly tales concerning the house started once more, however, no explanation for the macabre find has ever been offered.

Today Studley Park appears on a number of Websites as "Australia's most haunted building." There have also been several television series made there, including a program for Unreel Films, which recorded some interesting data. Their sound equipment certainly picked up some evidence, which suggested the voices associated with some of the rooms, but instead of the tones of either Ray Blackstone or Noel Gregory (the ghosts most commonly connected with the Park) they picked up the voice of a young girl. A medium, Debbie Malone, named the phantom as "Amelia" an 8-year-old girl who had been raped and brutalized in the room in which the sounds were heard, but could gather no more details. No record of such a person living at Studley Park exists. But who is to say that there are not more ghosts drifting about the building than those we already know about?

Can a building take on some of the senses of those who had built it and lived there? Does the feeling of oppression—the melancholy and dismal feelings—result, perhaps, from the frustrated dreams of William Payne who originally constructed Studley Park, or from the horror and grief following the tragic deaths of Ray Blackstone and Noel Gregory? Have some of these emotions been somehow absorbed into the very framework of the house? Perhaps some of the answers can only be found within the echoing rooms of what is, for some, Australia's most haunted house.

Wadi Rum

Southern Jordan

"The swarm of jinn is passing,
And it whirls hissing,
Old conifers, stirred by their flight,
Crackle like burning pine."
—Victor Hugo, *Les Djinns*

Perhaps our human world—the one that we perceive on a daily basis—somehow overlays another more shadowy type of reality, which somehow seeps through into our own at times, making us feel uncomfortable and ill at ease. This is an underlying tenet of the philosophy of certain Arab peoples—particularly that of the Bedouin—who believe that the spirit world is ever present, existing close to our own world, and always ready to make its presence known. Such intrusions are everywhere and the wise person has to be on his or her guard and recognize them when they occur.

In the deserts of Southern Jordan, the wind blows endlessly across vacant spaces stirring up tiny whirlwinds of sand and dust. According to the Bedouin peoples, these are manifestations of the *djinn,* forces from another world manifesting themselves in ours. The terms *djinn* or *djinii* are, according to those who know of such things, blanket ones, covering at least five major categories of spirits—jann, jinn, efreet, shaitan, and marid—although all of these are interchangeable, if required. They are creatures of pre-Islamic antiquity, which were later incorporated into Arabic religious teaching and are mentioned in the Holy Qur'an. Early Arabic works, such as Abou el-Hasan Ali al-Masudi's (896–956) *Meadows of Gold*, detail the distinction in orders of djinn and states that they were created contemporaneously with Adam and Eve. They are supposedly beings of air and smoke, having been forged by Allah from the *semoum* (*simmum),* the burning wind that blows across the desert places. Some thinkers have suggested that they are beings that are something between ghosts (ancestral spirits) and demons (things that have actually never been born), but there is no strict definition for them. A little less than angels, but slightly more than man, the djinn are envious of humankind who usurped their place in Allah's favor, and often seek to do them harm. For this reason, they have been banished to remote, desert places, far away from human settlements and cities where they can do little harm. In such places such as isolated graveyards, ancient ruins, and in deep and inaccessible caves (such as the Majlis al-Jinn—the Congress of the Spirits—a mysterious cave system in the Sultanate of Oman), they gather to plot the downfall of humankind. In ancient times, the djinn supposedly built cities in isolated locations where they could gather, and some of the remnants of these places still exist. Such a place is Wadi Rum in the southern Jordanian desert.

The desert lands to the east of the Gulf port of Aqaba are perhaps the most mysterious in the Middle East. A largely empty place and now occupied by Bedouin tribes, it has been the home of some passing but extremely ancient civilizations. One of these was the mysterious Nabatean culture that flourished between AD 37–100) and whose enigmatic trade-capital of Petra on the edge of Wadi Araba still stands as a tourist attraction to this day. But arguably, the most eerie and terrifying

of all the places in the eastern deserts is Wadi Rum, a remote valley that boasts a spectacular rock outcropping lying about 60 kilometers to the east of Aqaba. Also known as The Valley of the Moon, this depression, with its spectacular rock formations, is the largest wadi in all of Jordan. It is thought that the name "Rum" comes from ancient Aramaic and means "high or elevated." The highest part of the wadi is Mount Um Dami, which rises 1,800 feet above sea level. One section of the wadi, favored by rock-climbers, is the towering Jebel Rum, which is said to be one of the highest (if not *the* highest) peak in all of Jordan.

Wadi Rum has a long history of human occupation dating back to prehistoric times. The Khaz'ali Canyon contains ancient rock paintings that date back to possibly the 3rd or 4th centuries and perhaps even earlier. Many of these seem to show humans, camels, and antelopes, and mixed in among them are snatches of a strange written language that it is almost impossible to read. This, say the Bedouin of the area, is the tongue of the djinn themselves. It is clear, however, that Wadi Rum has been some sort of central location for many ancient cultures and that it has been a site of ancient veneration throughout the years.

There is no doubt that the wadi is a mystical place. Local fugara (Bedouin healers and sorcerers) and muquarribun (the Ghost Priests of an ancient Arabic tradition) claim that magics and forces from the dawn of time still resonate there, but what are its origins? While geologists may come up with a number of answers citing the age of rocks and the geographical strata of the surrounding desert, the Bedouin holy men know better. Wadi Rum, they say, is the site of a once great city built by the djinn from which they could control the land all the way west to the Gulf of Aqaba. From here, a number of djinn caliphs ruled through their witchcraft and magic conquering the early settlements of the frail humans nearby and enslaving them.

Their reign was ended by a powerful king of Israel who knew the incantations to defeat them. His name was Solomon, the wisest and most powerful of all Israelite monarchs, and he knew enough of their lore to bend the djinn to his will and force them to help build the Temple in Jerusalem. He destroyed their monsterous city with fire, leaving only the shattered remains that mark Wadi Rum. However, he wasn't able to destroy their influence entirely, and their baleful powers still linger on there. The djinn, scattered to the lonely desert places before Solomon's wrath, still consider the wadi to be their spiritual home, and will return there from time to time. It is then that the wadi is at its most dangerous, and humans should consider staying away. At least this is what the local Bedouin holy men say.

Because of its great and primal power, the wadi is also sacred to the Muquarribun. There are things hidden there, they say, which have been left over by the djinn from the very formation of the world. For instance, somewhere among the rock formations there is said to be a number of scrolls, known as the *Whispers of Angels* encased in brass cylinders, which contain certain Words of Power, known only to the djinn, which relate specifically to the formation of the Universe. These are words that Allah used to create things and which were written down by a category of djinn who overheard them. Yet, even if they were found they would be of no use to Mankind, as they are written in some form of prehistoric language. Even if they were to be translated, the knowledge contained therein is so powerful that it would almost certainly destroy the reader's mind and leave him or her a gibbering wreck. The only person who could read it, according to lore, is a great magician, well skilled in magic arts and with his head enclosed in a circlet of iron (curiously enough the same is said of some Icelandic and Scottish grimoires such as *The Red Book of Appin*). It is, however, best not to try to read these scrolls at all. According to tradition, the Ghost Priests frequently visit the site to converse with the djinn and learn further secrets from them—the wadi is often seen as the source of their power.

And, of course, such a significant geographical desert site features in Western literature as well. It is said that the wadi inspired the great Englishman, T.E. Lawrence to write his celebrated book *The Seven Pillars of Wisdom* (although Wadi Rum does not actually feature in the work). Indeed, as a British army officer, Lawrence was based at Wadi Rum during the Arab Revolt of 1916–17 and apparently found it a strangely eerie place. The main literary influence of the legends concerning Wadi Rum, however, has been on a much darker corpus of writing. This was reputedly the site of Irem, City of the Pillars, in the fiction of H.P. Lovecraft. This legendary and monstrous literary city mirrored many of the characteristics of the djinn-built metropolis at Wadi Rum. In Lovecraft's fiction, it is constructed by supernatural and terrible forces, such as the djinn themselves. It is unseen by many humans—"the nameless city that no man knoweth"—as are the traces of the ancient edifice at Wadi Rum. Both of these places were believed to contain a repository of abominable knowledge that would drive humans mad. Lovecraft's mad Arab soothsayer, Abdul Alhazerad, traveled to it in order to learn great mysteries there, in the same way that the Bedouin fugara and Muquarribun still travel to the wadi in order to increase their powers.

And there are those among such travelers who say that the djinn-city still exists invisibly in the desert, and that the sounds of the djinn who may still dwell there can be heard, howling. Of course, such sounds might be credited to the desert wind, echoing through the crannies and gullies of the place, but those who have heard "the call of the djinn" claim that there is an eerie, supernatural quality to the sound that cannot be fully explained away by attributing it to the natural elements.

"The sound was made even more terrifying," wrote correspondent Jan Vogel on an Internet travel site in 2005, "by the silence of the desert all around. It had the mournful wail of some lost soul, and I could well understand how the local Bedouin would claim it to be the cry of some supernatural desert being wandering through the waste."

Writing in his blog in 2007, Gavin from Glasgow describes the sound "… like a distant Greek Orthodox choir. If I was superstitious and hadn't benefitted from a sound scientific training, I would have thought it was the sound of devils shrieking in the darkness." To the local Bedouin, the idea of simple wind sounds is much too simplistic. For them, the sounds *are* indeed the voices of devils that still dwell there invisibly and often cry out to passers-by, seeking to draw them into their world. For them, the wadi is a place to be largely avoided and even many from the nearby settlement of Rum village will not go there, especially after nightfall!

So what lurks out there in the trackless Jordanian waste? Are there indeed the invisible remnants of a primal lost city, inhabited by ancient but powerful forces that have dwelt there since the dawn of time itself? And do they still have some sort of contact with the local witches and Ghost Priests who dwell close by? Perhaps the only way to find out is to go there. But it is probably best not to go at night or when the desert wind stirs the sands! Who knows what might well be lurking in the emptiness?

Warleggan

Bodmin Moor, England

"They were really quite sorry in their way for the lonely,
unpopular old fellow whom everybody shunned and at whom
all the dogs barked singularly."
—H.P. Lovecraft, *The Terrible Old Man*

Can the reported eccentricities of one individual contribute in some way to the "creepiness" of a particular location? Perhaps not on their own, but as a part of the geography, the history, and the overall "atmosphere" of a place, they can certainly evoke certain disturbing associations within us. Naturally, remote locations lend themselves to such feelings and seem to accentuate and add to the tales of certain strange individuals who have once lived there. Deep forests, bare mountains, or desolate moorland can often add to the feeling of unease, which we feel when listening to the tales concerning such people.

Bodmin Moor in Cornwall is such a desolate place. Here, stretches of bleak moorland are punctuated only by wreathes of mist that come and go along the lonely roads, which connect the scattered moorland communities, many of which are no more than small villages that have existed there for centuries. Because of the remoteness of their location, many of these villages exist in their own small worlds, each with their own histories and curiosities. This, of course, can be viewed by the traveler through the region as "quaint" and "charming"—and so it is—but sometimes there is a slightly darker edge to such traditions, and they have been tinged by some stranger individuals who have left their mark on local history.

The tiny village of Warleggan has existed out on the Moor for centuries with a church that is said to date back to Norman times. Up until 1818, it was one of the very few moorland churches with a spire, but it was struck by lightning and was never rebuilt. Although it has grown in recent years, Warleggan still remains a small place and is easily missed by those keeping to the main roads across the Moor. It is sometimes described as "the loneliest village on Bodmin." Presently dedicated to St. Bartholomew, it may have been built upon an old Celtic site (the outline of the graveyard follows a circular Celtic pattern) and the establishment of the place of worship there dates back to Norman times.

The church first appears in historical records around 1328 when the new priest there, John de Tremur, refused to live in the appointed clerical house on the grounds that he was a scholar (and therefore of a goodly and substantial background) and because his predecessors had allowed the house to fall into disrepair to the extent that it was almost a ruin. There was also a passing reference to certain beliefs and practices carried on in the locality against which the new priest seems to have taken a dim view and refused to be associated. No specification is given as to what these beliefs might be. Three years later, however, in 1331, de Tremur was expelled from his living and was excommunicated from the Church following an assault on one of the members of his congregation. There seems to have been *something* that infuriated the priest to the point where he almost killed the parishioner. He was succeeded by his nephew, Ralph de Tremur, who once again refused to come to Warleggan, but preferred to stay in Oxford where he was a scholar. Ralph de Tremur was an extremely learned man, being fluent in Cornish, Latin, French, and English. He did visit the church from time to time, but didn't seem to spend a lot of time there. In 1334, something happened, and the new church-man resigned and became a wandering cleric, traveling across Cornwall, openly denouncing all sorts of practices that he considered to be idolatrous and heathen. He was openly denounced as a heretic and a witch across Cornwall. But he was not done with Warleggan, for he returned to the village, robbed the priest there, and tried to burn down his house. He was arrested and taken to Exeter where he was placed before Bishop Grandisson. The outraged Bishop threatened to bring the matter to the attention of the Pope, but in the end did not do so. However, he denounced de Tremur from the pulpit—"O detestable tongue, more poisonous than that of a mad dog, which ought to be cut out by the surgeons of the Church and Crown and be chopped up and thrown to the pigs."

Evidences of older, more superstitious practices were evident in the church—for example, a "Devil's Door," through which the Infernal One could come and go (and be driven out), especially at times of baptisms, certainly existed in the North Wall during the 14th century, and there were whispers that rites and fes-tivals that were not strictly Christian were carried on within its precincts even as late at the 17th century.

It was around 1434 when the building was first associated with St. Barnabas, but there were still hints that strange rituals were being carried on there, although nothing specific is actually stated. However, the church now entered a period of relative stability with the rise of the Beare family—prominent landlords and mine-owners in the area. They built extensions to the church and added a deco-rated elvan baptismal font. Even so, the strange tales about the region continued. The church at Warleggan (like the neighbouring one at Temple) was also unusual in that it would allow marriages without either licence or banns being called. Consequently, couples who needed a speedy marriage for whatever reason often made their way there and the Bodmin phrase "sent to the moors" often means a hasty marriage.

Despite more stable ecclesiastical conditions, the relations between the rec-tors of Warleggan and their congregations were still sometimes difficult. In 1706, for instance, a French Huguenot named Daniel Baudris became rector and built a brew-house where strong drink was made—some locals greatly disapproved of this and of Baudris's firebrand sermons, which seemed to be at odds with his style of living. However, he made some important extensions to the church. Several subsequent rectors were also great exorcists and cast devils out from the surround-ing countryside. This was a time when supernatural prowess was attributed to may of the clergy in parts of Cornwall, most notably the celebrated Parson Polkinghorn of St. Ives, made famous by the folklorist William Botterell. Many of their names have been lost, although one may have been Parson Samuel Gurney, who succeeded Baudris, but who did not live in Warleggan—he had several livings in order to maintain his large and ever-expanding family. It is said that Gurney (if it was indeed he) cast out a number of ghosts that were tormenting people in the area and that some of the clergy were greatly feared because of their supernatural powers. However, generally speaking, the Rectors and people "rubbed along" together across the passing centuries.

The minister who really set his seal on Warleggan and who is forever is associated with the village arrived in 1931. Sixty-one-year-old Frederick Densham was unknown to anyone in the village or to the Parish Council, and he immediately aroused suspicions. The great Rectory of 13 rooms had stood empty for a time and a Methodist chapel was now thriving in the village—the Methodist faith, as the congregation were to find out, was one with which Densham had some sympathies. Indeed, he was the son of a Methodist minister (how and why he had become a minister in the Church of England is unknown) and had worked for a while in Whitechapel, London in a boys' home before travelling to Natal, Africa, in 1921 where he had championed the rights of "colored people" for a time, but to no great effect. However, it appears that while in Africa, he had espoused the teachings of Ghandi and may have become interested in Eastern mysticism. It is thought he applied to become a missionary in India, but was turned down, and giving up on any foreign work, returned to England to take over the parish at Warleggan.

From the outset, it was clear that Densham had never worked in a country parish and that he had few interpersonal skills. A deeply spiritual and aesthetic man, he was nonetheless dealing with stolid Cornish farmers—who had very dour dispositions—and a community which was very tightly knit and set in its ways. And he made no attempt to meet that community "halfway." There is no doubt that Frederick Densham was a highly educated and well-read man, but to the villagers, he appeared austere and self-important, treating them with an air bordering on disdain. And for all his grand learning, many on the church council thought that there was something suspicious about him. When he met with the officers of the parochial church council—a number of whom had held that position for many years—he made several suggestions, and when the others were slow to respond, he told them that his proposals were carried. And dissension was beaten down in a most high-handed manner. Following a number of contentious meetings, a number of members refused to attend the Council, Densham simply had their names struck from the Parish electoral rolls.

He then annoyed his neighbors by buying a litter of puppies, which he proceeded to raise at the Rectory. This totally disregarded the wishes of his parishioners, many of whom were sheep farmers and for whom dogs were a constant source of menace. The Rector said that he wanted the animals for company in the lonely Rectory and overrode all objections. The pups grew and became large and muscular dogs, which Densham claimed he needed for his own protection—thus implying that his congregation were not to be trusted. A couple of them seemed particularly fierce, including the Rector's favorite, which he named Ghandi. As the dogs grew, they seemed to become more aggressive, and it was not long until the sheep of certain farmers were savaged by the pack of dogs. The local story was that this was led by the Rector's dog Ghandi. A group of local farmers met with Densham, but the Rector airily brushed their protestations aside saying that *his* dogs would not be involved in such activities. The meeting marked a kind of turning point in relations between Densham and at least some of his congregation, and many of the farmers subsequently stayed away from the church. But there were other things that made the congregation slightly uneasy about the Rector.

Densham owned a large collection of books, some of which (as mentioned by those who had seen them) were not the sort of texts that an Anglican clergyman should be reading. The Rector had openly expressed a great interest in Eastern religions and some of his sermons reflected this, much to the discomfort of his listeners who had come to listen to an Anglican message. There were also hints that he had other works on pagan and folk religions—some of which might have been connected to Black Magic—and it was known that from these he copied pages of copious notes. Perhaps in some high academic circles, such things might have passed without remark, but in a small rural place such as Warleggan, his congregation felt distinctly uneasy.

In the meantime, the sheep worrying on the Moor continued and a deputation of farmers again met with the Rector. This time Densham, mindful of his dwindling congregation, was not quite so dismissive of their concerns. He offered them a compromise. Although not admitting that it was his dogs that were savaging sheep, he would build a perimeter fence all around the extensive Rectory grounds (which covered three and a half acres) to keep the hounds in. The congregation remained unmoved and so Densham began the work himself. This took a number of months, and at the end of it, more than 600 yards of barbed wire, more than 8 feet high, surrounded the property, keeping everything in and everyone out. The place now resembled a prison camp. Behind this Frederick Densham continued to study his dubious books and make his notes.

By now, his congregation had diminished quite considerably and in an effort to bring them back, Densham began to paint the church. The colors he chose were rather strange—reds and blues so deep that they had an almost medieval feel to them. As usual, he hadn't asked the church council for their approval (which would almost certainly have been denied), and proceeded to do the painting at night when his congregation was asleep. The following Sunday, one of the remaining members stood up and told the Rector that he had desecrated the

Lord's House and walked out, taking some others with him. This had no effect on Densham, who painted over the Church windows so thickly that little light could penetrate. His remaining parishioners asked for light in the building and in response, the Rector brought one candle. It must indeed have been an eerie sight to see the gloomy church lit by only a single light with Densham preaching to a handful of the faithful.

Matters came to a head in 1933 when the Rector closed the Sunday School. Locals assumed this was due to his "Eastern principles" and perhaps his pagan sympathies. He began to change the times of services in the Church in order to correspond with a "more natural order of things" (something which they took as being connected to paganism) and when he held a service at 3 a.m. on a Sunday morning, it was too much for the remainder of the congregation. They petitioned the Bishop, Dr. Walter Frere to have Densham removed. The Bishop, for some reason, took the step of meeting the congregation and Rector together. They met in the darkened church lit once again by only a solitary candle. Densham was accused of a number of things, including the closure of the Sunday School; that he had refused to hold services at convenient times; that he had converted Church property to his own use without any form of reference to the Church Committee; that he had threatened to sell the Church organ, which was a local memorial to several families who had fought in World War I; and that he had erected the now notorious barbed-wire fence around the Rectory. No mention was made of alleged witchcraft practices although the Secretary to the Church Council showed a letter in which Densham had threatened to kill him "by holy magic." Densham explained that this was a "misunderstanding"; that he was under no obligation to keep the Sunday School open and that the barbed-wire fence was only to restrain his dogs as the congregation had asked. The meeting ended with the Rector and the secretary shaking hands. The Bishop explained to the congregation that he could not remove Densham, as the Rector had broken no ecclesiastical law. He might be a bit eccentric and hold services at odd times, but he held a service every Sunday and fulfilled pastoral duties as he was required to do. Nevertheless, the vitriol of the congregation had shaken the Bishop and he suspected certain things about Densham, but couldn't prove them. He urged everyone to make a fresh start. The parishioners, however, had no intention of doing so and the last of the congregation left the Church and did not return for the duration of the Densham's Rectorship.

The Rector retreated behind his barbed wire, unwilling to meet his congregation. Some argued that he had been terribly hurt by the meeting. For centuries, Warleggan had been governed by three local landowners, but by the 1930s, their estates had been broken up and there was no real "squire" worth the name. It is argued that Densham thought that he, as Rector, should have filled the void left by the great estates, and that his congregation should simply accept his word as their new master. When they didn't, he ceased to have anything to do with them. He refused to visit the local shop and even had a Bodmin grocery roundsman call fortnightly to leave a box containing such items as cheese oats and butter at the Rectory gates. In accordance with his Eastern principles, he refused to eat meat, poultry, or fish, and he always ate only one meal a day, usually porridge. He grew a large rhododendron bank, which cut off his view of the village and became something of a recluse.

That is not to say, however, that Densham didn't have his supporters in the village. Some people tried to call upon him—Densham had a large oil drum placed at the Rectory gate which the delivery man would bang with a stick when he was delivering groceries—and some of the villagers banged on that to attract him down, but he seldom came. Some of those in the village wouldn't hear a bad word said against him—he was lonely and confused. They kept their eye on the one solitary chimney that could be seen above the rhododendrons and when they saw "the Rector's smoke" issuing from it, they knew he was well. He welcomed strangers to the Rectory, but for a great deal of the time, he wouldn't let any locals cross his threshold. A visiting clergyman from a nearby parish who called on him found him to be "cheerful and bright…a very solid man. A bit odd in his ways but quite pleasant." Densham now began to exhibit several odd characteristics. For example, he shunned the local wells and washed himself only in rainwater. And he refused to talk to people who had the smell of cigarette smoke on their breath. He began to paint each of the rooms in the Rectory with esoteric Biblical scenes—mainly from the book of Revelation, but featuring the drunkenness of Noah and the supernatural translation of Enoch. And he wrote more and more, accumulating great files of material.

By then, the Rectory was in a rather dangerous condition and this was not helped by Densham's attempts at do-it-yourself modernization. Damp and decay were now creeping all through the house and from his small stipend, Densham could not afford to make repairs. He wrote numerous letters to the District Council complaining about the rates and received a reply suggesting that if he found them too high, he should take in lodgers. He attempted to do this, but the Rectory was in such a dilapidated state and was filled with Densham's garish paintings that most prospective lodgers took one look and quickly decided against staying there. The fact that there was no electric light or running water in the place dissuaded some even from coming to view it. Gradually, the Rectory fell into even greater disrepair and the extensive grounds became badly overgrown. The branches of the trees on either side of the drive grew so long that they actually met and formed a barrier to any access, and the rhododendrons were now so prolific that they provided obstacles on their own.

As damp and decay took over the rooms, causing plaster to crack, Densham once again tried to get somebody to live with him. Suggesting that he get an organist to move into the Rectory, he wrote to a choir school in the Midlands and asked them to send an organist who would reside at the Rectory and train the church choir—which no longer existed. A young man was sent down and was taken aback at the wilderness which was the Warleggan Rectory. He found Densham extremely strange, and the conversations between the two hinged on things that the young man found unwholesome—such as human sacrifice and pagan worship. At night, when he retired to a room in which nobody had slept for years, he was locked in with a heavy bolt across the door. There seems little doubt that Densham was prepared to keep him a prisoner in the Rectory, but he relented and begged for forgiveness. Realizing that there was no choir to train and indeed no congregation to which he could play, the young man hurriedly left the following day, despite Densham's pleading to stay.

It was then wartime, and Densham made further changes to the Rectory before writing to the authorities to say that he would accept evacuees from London there. He claimed that he'd made a number of "modernizations" to the place that would suit young children, including the building of many bunk beds. The authorities came, took one look, and left, telling him that "because there was no woman present" they could not possibly consider him. Once again his plans were thwarted.

At the time it appears that Densham began to fixate on small children. Perhaps he thought that if he won them over, the parents would follow. So venturing out from his Rectory, he bought large bags of sweets in Bodmin and began to wander around the village, offering them to any children that he met. Of course, parents were incredibly suspicious and ordered their children to stay well away from him. There were rumors that he was trying to tempt children into the Rectory for ritualistic purposes. Fresh complaints were made to the Bishop but Densham argued that he was only trying to fulfil his pastoral duties with the young. He even spent some of his meager money in trying to construct a childrens' playground within the Rectory grounds. After his death, a cemented depression (a swimming pool), a large cartwheel (a merry-go-round), and several other items were found among the brambles and overgrown bushes. He also purchased a magic lantern, which he housed in an outside barn to give "cinematic displays" to the young folk. These were supposed to be themes from classical mythology and folklore, however, some of the slides were slightly nightmarish—Polyphemus with a gouged-out eye and a horrible-looking Gorgon, certainly not suitable viewing for young children. Densham, however, thought that this would give an added thrill to the experience and the whole episode somehow reflected the fictional lantern show given by the sinister Mr. Karswell in the M.R. James story *Casting the Runes*. There was a significant difference, however, because no child attended the Rector's show. Local mothers were unwilling to trust their offspring to the children's play area—let alone allow them to enter a darkened room with a man like Densham.

The Rector's behavior became more and more erratic. For a while, he locked up his own church on a Sunday and attended the local Methodist gathering. However, because he would not behave himself, he frequently leapt to his feet and harangued the minister when there was something he disagreed with. Either that or roar in an unknown and barbarous-sounding tongue, which disconcerted many of the other worshippers. In the end he was asked to leave and returned to the Rectory.

In the latter years, Densham faithfully kept up the Church Register. Significantly under *Attendance* is the common entry "No congregation at any service." Under *Rector's Remarks*, which was supposed to detail parochial activities, he simply recorded observations about the weather. However, he had a plan to furnish himself with a "congregation" of sorts. Accounts vary, but it is said that he made himself a series of cardboard figures which he placed in the pews and preached to them. It was always the same sermon, "The Devil as a roaring lion," except at Christmas when he preached on "God is Love." Others say that it was not cardboard figures at all—this they claim was no more than an invention of the novelist Daphne du Maurier, who lived in Cornwall from 1943 and who knew of Densham—and that he simply preached to cards bearing the names of former Rectors. Whatever they were, he referred to them in his journal as "a congregation of ghosts."

Not only this, but he arranged a crude speaker system in the bushes near the church. This was little more than a metal box connected to an old microphone by a series of wires, but it served to carry the Rector's voice preaching the same sermon over and over again each Sunday to the houses nearby. The few residents there were treated not only to the sermon, but also expositions of missionary life in India with the inclusion of the radio show *The Brains Trust*. Had it not been so pathetic, it might have been humorous. Many of the residents complained to the District Council and eventually the broadcasts stopped.

Densham now contented himself with his writing. He wrote file upon file of text, consulting some of the "strange books" that he kept about the Rectory. He changed the paintings on the walls of the Rectory rooms, showing far away scenes of Biblical lands with peculiar twists—such as Christ raising Lazarus at Bethany and the road to Emmaus where Christ had appeared to some followers. He also seemed to be more fearful of something—some say that he saw death approaching—and began to paint every door of the house with a cross and other religious symbols. He also broke his silence with the village and asked one good parishioner to come in to see him and light his stove for him (he was now becoming increasingly infirm) and perhaps do a little meager cooking. But the overwhelming feeling in that lonely Rectory was now one of fear.

From about 1951 onward, Densham had, from time to time, a peculiar audience at some of his services. The reclusive Rector had become something of a curiosity in America and occasionally some journalists and photographers would show up at the church to try to interview him. There were reporters for *Life Magazine* and the *Western Morning News*, as well as from some of the London papers, who also viewed him as a curiosity. They photographed him for a while as he harangued the local Methodists for their "Hellbound" ways, such as drinking and smoking, and as he preached to the empty church. Eventually though, even the press lost interest in him and the Rector retreated behind his rhododendrons and shut his Rectory doors once more.

He returned to writing, allegedly filling his files with material copied from "terrible books," drawing peculiar symbols on the doors. The rumor that the Rectory was haunted was now an accepted part of local folklore. But things were about to change.

One morning in 1953, some locals noticed that "the Rector's smoke" wasn't rising from the one chimney, which could be seen behind the high rhododendrons. Alarmed that something was wrong, several of them beat on the oil drum beside the gate, hoping that Densham would show himself, but he didn't. After calling the police, they went up to the overgrown Rectory and found him dead where he had fallen at the foot of the stairs. According to most accounts, there was a look of absolute terror on his face and his hands had been raised as if to ward something away. He had been dead for two days. The villagers inspected the church records, hoping to gain some clue. The last entry for the Sunday before simply read: "No wind, no rain, no sun, no congregation. Both stoves burned excellently." There was also a cryptic reference to another visitor named as Tom Webster who arrived at the Rectory at 3:10 p.m. on Sunday having travelled by British Rail. There was no record of him leaving. No trace of this individual or what his business with Densham might have been was discovered. Further searches of the house were made and it's alleged that there were other items found in some of the rooms that were quickly and quietly disposed of, although Densham's private papers were not touched. A day or two after the discovery, his brother arrived to take charge of his possessions. The man proved to be as taciturn as the Rector had been and reportedly spent several days carrying his brother's books and hundreds of files to the back of the Rectory where he created a great bonfire and burned them all before departing. In the back of the house was a study where every cubby hole had been filled with sheets of paper and scroll-like texts, all of which were taken out and destroyed. There were clearly some things that he did not wish other eyes to see.

Gradually scant traces of Densham's last hours began to emerge. There had been a basket of apples placed on the kitchen table, he would take to some of his parishioners. At some point he had gone upstairs—some speculated in order to die—but had never reached the top. He had fallen down dead and lay where he had been found. The cause of his death was given as a heart attack.

His brother never returned to finish clearing out the Rectory, and shortly after his death, some of the contents of the house were put to auction. None, however, gave any clue as to his mysterious life, and although many turned up to see, they felt no closer to their Rector than they had when he was alive. Densham had left specific written instructions for his burial and had constructed a "Garden of Remembrance" enclosed by laurels in the grounds of the Rectory where he was to be laid to rest. The locals ignored these and cremated his body, scattering his ashes in the official Garden of Remembrance in Plymouth. Neither his brother nor any member of his family attended the funeral, nor did any member of the Warleggan parish. In fact, only one mourner attended his funeral—his solicitor.

Warlaggan Church was whitewashed and the Rectory was sold. After Densham there was never another Rector in the parish, and today, the old house is let out as apartments. When they cleaned out the cellars, builders found several more sheets of paper, but these turned out to be no more than lecture notes and several lines of jokes. Frederick Densham had passed into history without much of a legacy.

And yet his shadow still hangs over Warleggan. Old people there still remember him and a number of residents claim to have seen his ghost—sometimes alone, sometimes with his dog—along the lanes around the present village. There are still tales of haunting in the old Rectory, and people still puzzle over what went on there. Following his death, another clergyman in a neighboring parish took over and the congregation returned in some measure to St. Bartholomew's, but some members still say that it was "never an *easy* church." Was Densham no more than a harmless, reclusive, and greatly misunderstood eccentric? Or within the walls of the Rectory did he use Eastern and pagan magics to call down something from beyond, which still somehow lingers in the quiet places of the village? And his strange character seems to have influenced those further afield. There have been several articles and fictional stories written about him, and in 2009, Mark Collicot's film *A Congregation of Ghosts* was shot in Cornwall. Although dead for more than 50 years, his strange influence still continues and may still have the power to chill us all!

Wavery Hills Sanatorium

Louisville, Kentucky

"If you listen carefully," whispered Beatrice putting her ear close to the door, "You can sometimes hear her moving about inside. She's on the other side of the door you know, listening all the time, trying to catch what's going on out here in the passage. She is awfully quiet during the daytime, but sometimes when you're in bed at night, you can hear her shouting and laughing in this room, even away across the house. I think that's when she frightens me the most."

—Harriet Burdon, *The Mad Woman's Room*

Many people, myself included, find hospitals to be frightening places. Maybe it's their associations with illness and death that chills us most. And no matter how modern the building, the frowning, sterile walls, and the strange, clinical smells often give us fear. And because of their connections with death—whether sudden or lingering—it is a small wonder that many hospitals have acquired a "haunted reputation" throughout the years.

One of the most haunted is the Waverly Hills Sanatorium, just outside Louisville, Kentucky. Not only is this one of the most troubled hospital sites in the United States, but it is also described as "one of the most haunted buildings in America." And yet, as haunted buildings go, Waverly Hills is fairly new, only dating back as far as 1910. That, of course, does not detract from its creepiness.

The name was given to the area by Major Thomas H. Hayes, who purchased the land on which the hospital now stands, in 1883. A fervent believer in education, Hayes established a one-room schoolhouse for his two daughters and some other children on what was then known as Paige's Lane, and employed Miss Lizzie Lee Harris as a teacher. Miss Lizzie had a particular fondness for the novels of the great Scottish author Sir Walter Scott, and named the school The Waverley School after one of them. Hayes liked the name and it became official. When they took over the land in the early 1900s, the Board of the Hospital kept the name, although when the second "e" was dropped and it became Waverly Hills is unknown.

In 1911, Jefferson County was ravaged by what became known as "the White Plague" (tuberculosis). A great majority of the cases were in the Louisville area, which was particularly low-lying and swampy—a perfect breeding ground for the tuberculosis bacteria—and to try and contain the contagion, the city authorities built a rough wooden facility in which patients could be housed. There were, however, plans to build a more permanent hospital. Throughout 1911, work was hampered by financial wrangling and political manoeuvring, so the earliest patients were transferred to a new, temporary institution at Waverly Hills pending completion of a hospital in Louisville. Some of the structures were no more than wooden cabins, some were even tents, and the whole area had a very temporary feel about it.

Political and financial dealing nevertheless continued, and with the new hospital still not completed, more and more patients were transferred to the Waverly Hills site. Initially, the institution had been set up to deal with first-stage pulmonary tuberculosis, but advanced cases were being sent there. By December 1912, new wings were added to accommodate another 50 patients, all of whom were classed as "advanced cases." In 1916, a children's pavilion added yet another 40 beds. By that time, Waverly Hills was being classed as a "capacity hospital" and boasted around 130 patients. However, it is not known if this was actually a true figure, as building continued apace with the building of laboratories and extra spaces. In fact, the hospital seemed to grow a little bigger each year. Meanwhile, rumors began in the surrounding countryside. It was said that Waverly Hills was secretly an "experimental hospital" where doctors were experimenting on the terminally ill in secret additional structures to try to find a cure for the disease which was blighting parts of the state.

In 1924, it was becoming apparent that Waverly Hills would no longer be regarded as a "temporary hospital," and that a more permanent structure should be built. A five-story building was proposed, and it would include a number of facilities to house long-term sufferers of tuberculosis in the Louisville area, which would hold more than 400 patients. This opened on October 17th, 1926, and was certainly an imposing building. However, rumors about what was going on there still persisted. The secret laboratories, it was said, had now become formalized and more sophisticated, and terminal patients were being experimented upon there daily by certain members of staff.

In certain cases of tuberculosis, the disease had affected the brain of the patient and madness had set in. A special "mad ward" was rumored to exist within the hospital where the insane were kept. Many of these people were from poor families who simply deposited them at Waverly to be rid of them, so this ward in particular was said to be a rich picking ground for doctors who wished to medically experiment with patients. If they died, who would miss them?

Waverly ran as a tuberculosis hospital until the 1960s. However, in 1943, the widespread use of streptomycin led to a decline in numbers suffering from the disease. Although it remained open throughout the 1940s and 50s, the numbers of patients grew less and less, and areas of the building were largely abandoned. Or were they? Local legends suggested that even more medical experiments went on there in the now "empty" wards and laboratories, particularly during the latter years of World War II. However in June 1962, Waverly Hills finally bowed to the inevitable and closed its doors as a tuberculosis hospital with the remaining inmates being transferred to the City Hospital in Louisville.

It didn't stay closed for long though. At the end of 1962, it reopened again as Woodhaven Geriatric Home, which would remain in operation until 1981. Although it was classed as a "geriatric hospital" stories suggested that it was in fact an asylum for the confused and mentally ill. After all, it did have a "mad ward." People who were too disturbing or too violent to be housed in regular mental facilities were shipped there to be kept away from public gaze. In 1981, amid allegations of patient abuse, Woodhaven Medical Services, who owned the building, closed it down once more.

By then, the hospital was a center of rumor and story. There were tales of a "death tunnel" that ran beneath it. It ran from the first floor down to an exit at the bottom of the hill on which the hospital stood. One side of the passageway comprised a flight of steps, the other, a small rail and a cart powered by a motorized cable. Staff often used this tunnel to come and go without having to walk up a steep and dangerous hill—and also without being seen from the hospital itself. According to Woodhaven Services, this had been built during the time of the tuberculosis hospital and had originally been used to transport supplies. During the height of the tuberculosis outbreaks, there were constant deaths at the hospital and the sight of bodies being taken out—sometimes on a daily basis—was upsetting for some of the other patients. Therefore, the "death rail" was used to discreetly remove bodies from some of the wards and take them to town for transport to Louisville without being seen. There were those who said that this "railroad" was used by some doctors to dispose of the bodies of those who had died during illegal experiments in the hospital.

And, of course, there were stories of the unquiet dead roaming the corridors at night, especially near what had been "the mad ward." Here, insane phantoms lurked among the shadows, ready to threaten unsuspecting nurses as they passed. Some of these could be quite terrifying to look at—gibbering and gesticulating in an awful manner before vanishing into the dark. One of those most frequently seen is that of an old woman with long, straggly white hair; staring insane eyes; and dressed in a blood-stained tunic with metal cuffs. She may have been a particularly violent inmate of the geriatric hospital who needed to be restrained and is waiting for her family to come and take her home. She is still waiting, and in the dark of the night, presents a truly terrifying sight. And in the darkness, from time to time, the screams and the groans of the former inmates—some demanding to be let out, some simply shouting in pain from the alleged experiments, can be heard, far away and echoing across the building

But the most persistent legend concerns Room 502. In 1928, with the tubercular fever raging at its height, a young nurse was found hanging from one of the beams. Why she took her own life is unknown, but she may have been unmarried and pregnant. Later, in 1932, another nurse supposedly jumped to her death from the roof of the building after spending some time in Room 502. Thos who have visited the room say that there is a definite air of depression within its walls, which has affected them greatly. It is as if a baleful presence lurks there, pushing those who enter there toward suicidal thoughts.

In 1983, there were plans to turn the hospital into a minimum security prison. It was bought by Clifford Todd for around $305,000 with the idea of developing it for those purposes, but it was swiftly dropped when the neighbors started

protesting. Todd and his partner Milton Thompson then considered turning it into apartments, but that plan soon fell through as well. One of the problems that the developers experienced was finding night watchmen to remain in the building during hours of darkness. Few local men could be persuaded to keep watch there because of the voices and sounds that were allegedly heard, and the eerie feeling that many experienced there. Electrical equipment switched itself off and on and curious voices were heard on walkie-talkies carried by the guards—voices that didn't sound completely sane. After a great deal of legal and financial wrangling the developers called it a day and sold the property on.

In 1996, its next buyer was the Christ the Redeemer Foundation who planned to turn it into a religious sanctuary with a statue of Jesus, which would rival the one on Corcovado Mountain above Rio de Janeiro. The main building would form a complex in which there would be a church, theater, and even a gift shop. Some work began, but once again, odd voices were heard, equipment went missing, and a number of small accidents occurred, suggesting ghostly goings-on. The idea that the place might be haunted had a direct affect on fund-raising for the project. In fact, funding fell away and in 1997, the enterprise was abandoned.

Since 2008, there have been plans to turn Waverly Hills into a hotel complex. At present, the site is closed off with guards and security cameras at various points. But the ghostly stories about it still circulate—particularly about the insane ghosts that are supposed to haunt its corridors. It was featured on the Fox Family Channel's *Scariest Places on Earth*, on the Travel Channel's *Ghost Adventures*, and Zone Reality's *Creepy*, as well as the Syfy Channel and the British Television series *Most Haunted*. There has even been a strip in a French comic book (*Pandemonium* by Christophe Bec) concerning supernatural goings-on in Waverly Hills.

Do the ghosts of the ill or insane still haunt the former hospital? If you were really interested, you could always travel to Louisville to find out. Only, for your own sanity, it's perhaps best not to go at night!

Winchester Mystery House

San Jose, California

"...I need only describe the spectre which had
haunted my midnight pillow."
—Mary Wollstonecraft Shelley

A sad, strange woman, perpetually haunted by ghosts; an eerie house, the building of which has no end; the legacy of a violent weapon. All of these elements come together at the Winchester Mystery House. Is this bizarre building truly a monument to the dead, or simply the crazed fancy of a terrified woman who imagined herself hounded by forces from another world? Do phantoms *really* prowl its maze-like corridors or lurk in the furthest corners of its countless rooms? Or is it all simply fevered imagination and delusion?

In a sense, the history of the Winchester House in the Santa Clara Valley, is just as bizarre and intriguing as the building itself. It began in 1839 with the birth of a baby girl to Leonard and Sarah Pardee in New Haven, Connecticut, a child whom they named Sarah. The Pardees were wealthy people and Sarah grew up determined to become a young lady of society—a task which she set about with some success. She was soon the talk of New Haven society as a lady of charm, wit, and elegance. Diminutive in stature, she was nevertheless an exceptionally gifted musician and fluent in a number of languages. She had a number of suitors, most of whom proposed marriage, but she had her eye set on one man—William Wirt Winchester. William was another prominent New Haven figure and the son of a prosperous shirt manufacturer, Oliver Winchester. In 1857, he took over some assets from a firm that owed him money—the Volcanic Repeater Company, a weapons firm that made a rifle with a lever mechanism for loading bullets directly into the breach. This weapon was an improvement on other firearms of the day, but Winchester believed that it could be developed further. The new company, which bore his name developed the Henry Repeater Rifle in 1860, that attached a tubular magazine to the firing barrel, which made it easier and faster to reload. Sales of the new weapon boomed, but were aided by the advent of the American Civil War. Indeed, it became the weapon of choice for the Northern troops throughout the course of the conflict. Sarah and William were married in New Haven on September 30th, 1862, as the rifle went into full-scale production.

With the war ended and an immense fortune amassed, William and Sarah settled down into married life and began to think about a family. On July 15th, 1866, Sarah gave birth to a daughter named Annie Pardee Winchester. After she was born, she contracted a mysterious infant disease that caused her body to waste away. Doctors were baffled. The baby died on July 24th, leaving Sarah devastated. Always of a delicate disposition, she actually veered toward madness at the time, but she had the best medical attention and rallied to some extent. She shut herself away and refused to see anyone, including her own husband, spending some periods in institutions. She would remain this way for almost 10 years and would never have another child.

Shortly after she finally returned home, another tragedy struck. On March 7th, 1881, William, now the heir to the Winchester fortune, contracted pulmonary tuberculosis and died. Upon his death, Sarah became the sole beneficiary of the Winchester Company, inheriting in excess of $20 million, which was an unbelievable sum that would set her up for life. And from the Winchester Repeating Arms Company, she received roughly $1,000 per day (non-taxable), which made her one of America's richest women at the time.

But despite all her unimaginable wealth, Sarah continued to grieve both for her husband and her lost child. She sank further and further into depression and began to alarm both her friends and family—one of whom suggested that she should consult a spiritualist medium in order to make contact with those she loved. The medium gave her a chilling message. She was under a curse, as was her family, resulting from the creation of the Winchester Rifle and the money she had made from it. This took away both her daughter and her husband, who would never rest until reparations were made. The ghosts of those who had been killed by the weapon were now seeking vengeance, and soon she would be consumed by their curse as well. What could she do? She must sell all her property in New Haven and travel west into the setting sun. The spirits of her husband and daughter would act as her guides, and when she found a place in which she was to settle, she would recognize it. If these instructions were not carried out, she would die.

Sarah followed the instructions and sold up her property in New Haven, heading west toward California. In 1884, she reached the Santa Clara Valley where she found a large, six-bedroom house already under construction. It was being built by a Doctor Caldwell in order to house his large family. The land around it amounted to 162 acres, which gave a great deal of room for expansion. Sarah convinced the doctor to sell her both the house and the land. She then threw away all previous building plans and began on her own project, building wherever she wanted to. She employed local craftsmen and builders and they changed, altered, built, and rebuilt to Sarah's own increasingly bizarre specifications. They demolished one section of the house, then rebuilt it, and then demolished it again. This went on for the next 36 years, during which time Sarah kept 22 carpenters at work in almost 24-hour service. They worked throughout both the day and night and the sound of sawing and hammering was to be heard at all hours.

A railway line was constructed to bring materials and furniture to the house—money was no object to Sarah—and the building grew from six to 26 rooms as the construction work continued. Sarah claimed to be guided by the spirit of her late husband, whether it was directly or through dreams, and each morning would turn up with a hand-drawn map, which she presented to the building foreman, detailing her ideas for the day. Although she claimed to have no real plan, she showed a definite aptitude for planning and construction work. When the plans didn't work out, Sarah just had the work demolished and began again. Rooms were added to and then turned into wings as the house grew and grew. Towers were added, and eventually, the house grew to a staggering seven stories. The interior was madness. There were 47 fireplaces in the rooms, but many could not be lit because the chimneys stopped short of the ceilings; cupboards opened into completely blank walls, staircases led nowhere or turned back on themselves, and three elevators were installed between floors, but only worked sporadically. Some of the doors leading out of the rooms dangerously opened into steep drops; corridors twisted in circles; skylights were arranged in doubles while some of the bathrooms and toilets had clear glass doors. The posts at the bottom of some of the staircases had been put in upside down and some of the grander doors were only ornamental and opened onto plastered walls.

There was a recurrent theme of the number 13 throughout the house, a number which Sarah considered to be mystical and important. There were, for example, 13 panes of glass in each window, wooden walls had 13 panels in each, many of the floors contained 13 sections. Nearly every staircase had 13 steps (one particular staircase had 42 steps—a multiple of 13—but each step was only 2 inches high—the staircase itself led nowhere); some of the rooms had 13 windows and the greenhouse had 13 cupolas.

What was Sarah's plan behind such a bizarre dwelling? She believed that this house was being constructed as living quarters for all the ghosts that had been killed through the use of the Winchester Rifle and who were trying to take vengeance on her. Because the number of such phantoms seemed to be endless, so was the building of the house itself. Using some ancient Eastern logic, she deliberately designed the corridors and staircases in a haphazard and maze-like style to confuse the ghosts who she believed were always around her. She lived in one part of the building, well away from where she perceived these ghosts to be, seeing nobody except the servants and the workmen.

Still, the house grew, and by 1906, it had reached an amazing seven stories. Late at night, Sarah would throw all its windows open (presumably to let the spirits out into the wider world) and would return to play on a grand piano that she had brought to the mansion. She would often play all through the night and although some people complained, many found it rather beautiful, as she was an accomplished pianist.

In 1906, California was shaken by a great earthquake centring on the San Francisco region, with aftershocks for many days afterward in various parts of the state. Great portions of the bizarre house fell and were reduced to rubble. The three uppermost floors had collapsed into the gardens and would not be rebuilt.

One of the bedrooms—where Sarah was actually sleeping—shifted and trapped her inside. Although rescued, she was now convinced that the earthquake was the work of the spirits who were furious that she was contemplating finishing the building of the place. She boarded up part of the house, which would not be completed, trapping (or so she believed) the spirits that were there inside. In order to confuse the vengeful spirits even further, she kept moving the place in which she lived around the remaining building, and in the end, nobody knew where she lived along the eerie corridors. In actual fact, the strange structure had fared much better in the earthquake than many of the houses around about and although it was a labor for the workmen to restore part of it, it was not as bad as it might have been. The expansion of the house began once more at a slightly brisker pace. Chimneys were built all over the place, although they appear to have served no purpose. Although, according to Sarah, the spirits came and went through them, entering and leaving the building by that route. The other thing she now forbade was for any mirrors to be installed in the mansion in case the spirits became trapped in their reflective surfaces. In the end, there were only two mirrors in the whole house.

Her behavior became wilder and wilder. It appeared that she seldom slept, but sat up all night, playing music on the piano or else wandering the twisting corridors and vacant rooms of the place talking to (or more likely shouting at) the spirits. On September 24th, 1922, she retired to bed in some remote part of the house and in the early hours of the following morning she died, at the age of 83. For many years, most of her business interests had been handled by her niece Frances Marriot, who became her main beneficiary as far as her house and possessions were concerned. It came as some surprise to find out that, despite her allegedly vast fortune, Sarah had been close to bankruptcy at the time of her death. This was partly due to the monies that she had squandered on the house, a series of bad investments, and outright stealing from her account by relatives (including Frances). There were rumors, however, that she herself had removed part of her money from bank accounts on the advice of the spirits, and that it was hidden somewhere in the house, together with a set of solid gold tableware, which she used for entertaining the spirits. Relatives, anxious for a share of the money, began to hunt everywhere, looking for secret cupboards where a fortune might have been stashed. They opened a number of concealed safes, but found nothing—just old newspaper reports concerning the death of her husband, underwear, several old photographs, a lock of Annie's baby hair, old baler twine and fishing lines, and several pairs of shoes. If the fortune was there, it remains there to this day.

Everything that could be removed from the mysterious house was removed, and the building was sold by the family, still trying to make their money out of Sarah's death. It was bought by a group of investors who wanted to turn it into a tourist attraction. One of the first people to enter the place was the American cartoonist and collector of the bizarre Robert LeRoy Ripley, famous for *Ripley's Believe It Or Not*. Ripley is believed to have bought some of Sarah's possessions, which he briefly exhibited in his Odditorium in Hollywood together with a small plaque about their previous owner. He certainly wrote about the house and Sarah's strange life in several of his newspaper columns. When it was put up for sale, the house was advertised as having 148 rooms, but no one could be sure (even to this day, nobody is sure *exactly* how many rooms it contains—each time they are counted, a different total comes up). Removal men got lost in the labyrinthine corridors, and it took several weeks just to get the furniture out of the place. Many spoke of hearing voices and whispers all through the place and nobody would work in the old house after dark. Footfalls echoed in seemingly empty rooms terrifying those who passed by, and presences were sensed along the twisting corridors and on the staircases. Today, the building is designated a California Historical Landmark and is the property of the State Parks Service whose literature simply describes it as having "an unknown number of rooms." No mention is made of ghosts.

But do phantoms actually walk there or is the bizarre structure no more than a monument to madness, built by unimaginable wealth in insane hands? Mediums have come to the house and have declared that they can still sense ghosts in some of the rooms. Most of these claims have been dismissed, but according to some tourists there have been "eerie sensations" within the house and several people have described a mysterious and eerie figure passing along some of the corridors. This figure had been subsequently identified as Sarah Winchester herself, the viewers could not have known. There have also been stories of cold spots, of voices in some of the empty rooms, of artifacts that move of their own accord, and of doors that open and close by themselves. There is no doubt that the sheer scale and bizarre history of the house lends credence to such stories, but what if they're true? What if the Winchester Mystery House is actually the biggest haunted house in the world? Perhaps it's worth taking a visit to find out. However, be careful that you don't get lost amongst its myriad rooms! The spirits might be waiting for you!

Tumbulagang

Tarlung Valley
Tibet

"'Not that room.' Miss Hammond clasped her lace-covered hands together so tightly I feared that she would break her skin and make them bleed. 'Oh my God, not *that* room. Don't go in there, I entreat you.'"
—Mrs. J.E. Howard, *The Shuttered Room*

During the early 20th century nowhere was as mysterious or as mystical as distant Tibet. Shut away among the towering Himalayas, this remote country took on a certain mystique of its own. In isolated and almost inaccessible monasteries deep in the country were secrets older than the world itself, and here, lamas (priests and monks) regularly used powers that were beyond the scope of most mortals. The Communist Chinese invasion of Tibet on October 5th, 1950, and the closing of its borders only served to add to its mystery. During the late 1940s, the 1950s, and the mid-1960s, Tibet and its lamaseries often became a place of pilgrimage for those seeking mystical adventures and for the rebellious youth of the time. The so-called "hippy trail to the East" ended in the city of Kathmandu in the neighbouring country of Nepal, and many who came there also hoped that they might take the Old Lhasa Road to the capital of remote Tibet. Chinese border guards invariably thought otherwise. And yet, the tales that came to the west from this mysterious land only increased and grew wilder. As the 1960s/1970s discovered writers such as H.P. Lovecraft and other visionaries of the Cthulhu Mythos, many became even more convinced that extremely ancient secrets were concealed somewhere among the cloudy monasteries.

What more spectacular place to house such ancient mysteries than the Yumbulagang Monastery (Yumbu Lhakang), reputed to be Tibet's oldest extant building? Perched on the top of a steep cliff and overlooking the Yarlung Valley, the Yumbulagang is every inch what a mysterious Tibetan monastery is supposed to look like. According to various and diverse traditions within the country, the monastery was built as a palace for Nyatri Tsenpo, who was the first king of Tibet of the so-called Yarlung Dynasty. He reigned around AD 127, and his name appears in both the Bon (a pre-Buddhist faith in Tibet that centered on the personality of a divine king, yet contained many Buddhist characteristics) and Buddhism. According to Bon legend, he descended from the Heavens by a golden rope onto Yalashangbo, a dome-shaped mountain in northwest Tibet, which was sacred to the surrounding people. The Tibetans welcomed him and made him their king. He had certain physical peculiarities—for example, his hands were webbed and his eyelids closed from the bottom of his eyes, not the top. This made the Tibetans also believe that he was a god, and they worshipped him as such. He was also immortal, but was brought up to Heaven once more by the same golden rope which had brought him to earth. He had also established a line of immortal kings, all of which were taken up into the clouds by various ropes—both gold and silver. His name reflects his inhuman ancestry and means "a sovereign enthroned from the neck" (in some versions of his legend, his neck is said to have included fish-like gills). They built the Yumbulagang in Southern Tibet as his Palace.

The 28th King of the Yarlung Dynasty (it is possible that prior to the establishment of the Tibetan Empire, these kings did not rule all of Tibet, but only the Yarlung region), he was Lha Thothori Nyantsen (the prefix Lha denotes that he is a sky god) who ruled around the late 600s. It is possible that he was an actual person, as he is mentioned in certain Chinese texts. During his reign, a golden dome (or *stupa*), together with a massive jewel, and a *sutra* (a volume of aphoristic sayings) that no one could read all fell from the skies in the vicinity of the Yumbulagang. The jewel and the sutra were taken in to the building and were stored in a secret room to which no one had access. At the same time, a mighty voice from the Heavens announced that "within five generations shall come one who can understand the meaning of the Sutra and the significance of the jewel." So far this person (if it is a person) has not appeared.

The palace became a Gelugpa (Yellow Hat—a branch of Tibetan Buddhism) teaching monastery during the reign of the 5th Dalai Lama, Lobsang Gyatso in the 17th century. Today, it is something of a tourist attraction and photos of it appear all across the Internet. However, strange stories about it still persist, adding to its mystery and eeriness.

For instance, there are said to be a number of secret chambers hidden away within its confines where no man is allowed to go, and in one of these is a being that no man can look upon. The construction of the building would seem to lend itself to such an idea. It is built in two sections—the front being a high, three-story building, while the rear portion is built like a tower, containing a number of rooms in which various statues and shrines are kept. These were said to include the effigies of King Neichi, first king of Tibet, and also of Songtsan Gampo, founder of the Tibetan Empire. The legend of Nyatri Tsenpo is said to disguise an even deeper ancient truth concerning ancient beings. Might the idea that an ancient "king" descended from the skies on a golden rope (or a golden ladder) be a disguised code for something that was unworldly and held within the monastery? Perhaps something else came from the skies, or perhaps some being has been confined there since the early days of the world. No one knows where these particular chambers are or what is confined there, but it is said that the mere sight of it is enough to drive a man mad and shake our deeply held beliefs about the origins of the Universe. There is an old tale from this area that the Head Lamas of the monastery would only enter the rear sections of the building after completing certain rituals and uttering certain protective incantations. Only then would their sanity be protected from whatever they saw within the area. Could this truly be something in the style of H.P. Lovecraft?

It is certainly an intriguing legend that has exercised many imaginations in the West. Indeed, one of those whose interest it piqued was the Nazi leader Adolph

Hitler. Hitler was interested in the ancient origins of races and in the primal world in general—believing that the Aryan race may have come from some prehistoric and forgotten source. His theories enthused some of his followers, in particular Heinrich Himmler, who became fascinated by Asian mysticism. Himmler became friends with the German zoologist and explorer Ernst Schafer who had conducted a number of expeditions into the Himalayas with the intention of exploring great parts of Tibet. Schafer indicated to Himmler that he wished to mount another expedition to the country and this was funded in part by the German Cultural Department on the understanding that it would conduct certain experimentation and investigations for the German government. According to legend, part of the "investigations" was to visit the Yumbulagang Monastery and negotiate a way into the secret chamber in order to prepare a report on what was there for the Nazi High Command. This specific order was said to come directly from Hitler himself. In order to give the expedition a quasi-military and official flavor, Schafer was given a position in the Nazi SS. The expedition took place between May 1938 and August 1939.

In January 1939, the team reached the Tibetan capital of Lhasa where they were permitted to remain for two months, studying culture, religion, and agriculture, as well as meeting Tibetan nobles. At the end of the two months, they set out on what appears to be the most secretive aspect of their mission—to the Yarlung Valley and the Yumbulagang monastery. This was, at the time, a very mysterious area and one to which previous British expeditions to Tibet had sought entry, but had been refused. What transpired within the Monastery is unknown, but the team left the area in great haste after they had visited it—the reason for this was given as being a swift return to Germany because of the approaching war. But was that the real reason? Stories that have developed around the visit to the Yarlung Valley state that although the German expeditioners were not taken into the hidden room or rooms, they were, nevertheless, shown "a great secret," which shook the entire expedition that eventually caused them to hurriedly leave Tibet. It is also said that a report was certainly sent by Schafer directly to Hitler in Berlin but that the report was heavily sealed and for the eyes of the Fuhrer only. What became of that report is unknown and its contents still remain a secret. However, many of his acquaintances say that Ernst Schafer was never comfortable in confined spaces or closed rooms after his return from Tibet. What was that "great secret" that Schafer was shown? No one knows, for he never spoke of it afterward and it died with him in 1992.

The expedition is often confused with the Nanga Parbat Expedition, which was in the region at the same time (May 1939–August 1939). This was essentially a mountaineering expedition that included Heinrich Harrer, a renowned Alpinist (and member of the SS Alpine Unit), and wanted to conquer Nanga Parbat (the name means Naked Peak), a killer mountain in the Himalayas that Harrer was determined to climb. However, it's thought that the expedition had been commissioned by the Fuhrer to look into other things besides climbing mountains. There was some speculation that the expedition leader, Peter Aufschnater, had been directed to collect a number of tales, especially those concerning what might be housed in the Yumbulagang and convey these back to Berlin upon his return. Whether this was done or not is unclear, as the expedition was captured by British forces under the command of Major General Alan Van Dyke, patrolling the mountains at the outbreak of World War II in October 1939. They managed to escape, although Harrer was recaptured, but managed to escape yet again. He arrived with Aufschnater in Tibet once more in 1944, travelling to Lhasa, where he lived until the Chinese arrival early in 1951. If he had brought back some of the tales concerning Yumbulagang, they remain in an archive somewhere in Germany and probably have since been lost.

So, although the monastery looks picturesque and in the middle of a breathtaking location does it hold a darker and more spectacular secret? There is a tale of an Italian explorer who visited the monastery in the 1920s (before the Nazi expedition) and who became friends with the Head Lama. It was said that, on his own insistence, he was taken into the secret room by the lamas. He turned up in Kathmandu in Nepal many months later, having fled the place along the Lhasa Road, raving and out of his mind. He never recovered his senses. His name is not given, but the story is said to be true. It is also said that this was the story that piqued Hitler's curiosity about Yumbulagang and prompted him to take a personal interest in Ernst Schafer's expedition.

What, then, lurks within the secret chambers of the ancient monastery? A spaceman from another world; some remote ancestor from which we are descended; something else too hideous to view? The answer may lie in a lost dossier from the 1930s, lying somewhere in Germany. But it's certainly enough to send a shiver along your spine.

Conclusion

"Some people do not believe in ghosts. For that matter
some people do not believe in anything."
—Mrs. J.H. Riddell, *The Open Door*

And so we reach the end of our journey. The choice of locations was, I admit, wholly arbitrary on my part, so I hope you found something truly creepy among them. It was a tough choice, and I could have filled another book of the same length with other places. Although they held certain macabre attractions, I tried to stay away from sites where really horrific acts had taken place such as Plainsville, Wisconsin (the home of the deranged serial killer Ed Gein) or areas of Crawley, London (the haunt of the vampire-killer John George Haigh), or even the gas chambers of the Nazi concentration camps in which millions of Jews and others were slaughtered. These places evoke responses in us, but perhaps the origins of these responses are of a rather different nature than that of genuine "creepiness." One of the most "creepy" feelings I have ever had was when I stood in the Bergen-Belsen Concentration Camp in northwestern Germany. I had been giving a talk with some colleagues in Berlin and had traveled north to the camp on a free day. As I stood in the open yard of the camp, I experienced something of a shiver running down my spine. But that sensation came not from the thrill of unease, but from one of utter horror and revulsion at what had happened within that location. Was it a feeling of "creepiness"? Yes and no. Probably something much more visceral, something lacking the subtlety of unease and uncertainty. Maybe that's why I enjoy the old ghostly movies of yesteryear a bit more than the gory horror flicks of today, and why I tend to read more of the older better-crafted tales of bygone authors than the more modern-day splatter stories. But I hope that my choice of places has fascinated you while at the same time sending a shiver along your spine.

So what have we learned about the nature of "creepiness" in our travels? First, that there's perhaps no real definition for the feeling and that it can mean different things to different people. It's a response, certainly, but maybe each person responds in a different way. And that the sensation/response is a very complex one. It's a bit more sophisticated than imagining that something or somebody may be lurking under your bed or in the wardrobe as you did when a child (although that may well be at least a part of it). It's more about responding to the *context* in which you find yourself. Although it is, I think, certainly a physical sensation, it is also one which relies on our mental and imaginative faculties. We are aware of the history of and/or the traditions concerning the site and, given this knowledge, we can imagine what might happen to us or what we might experience there. Of course, the very setting or association of the place itself may help—the lonely house, the isolated island, the remote monastery, the spectral castle, or the connection with someone sinister or obviously weird—but part of the feeling must derive from our own mental and imaginative activity. It relies on the notion of what we *perceive* might occur. This is what, I think, differentiates the "creepy" feeling from the basic stomach-turning schlock horror response to some of today's movies, television, and books, which would appear to have become something of a staple in what passes for modern-day "horror."

Secondly, "creepiness" may require a certain *attitude* in order to be effective. You may well have read through this book and found some of the stories and places interesting—you may even have said "I really must go there at some point, as I'd like to see that"—without experiencing any sort of chill along your spine. Maybe (and I'm willing to acknowledge the possibility) you bought this book as a kind of travel guide to unusual holiday places. In which case, you might have enjoyed reading about some of the sites—they may even have made you think—but won't really have experienced that "creepy thrill." Others of you might have been scared out of your wits. As with any other response, "that creepy feeling" requires some form of willing engagement at various levels. If you deliberately dismiss or shut out the possibility of this engagement, then such places will usually leave you cold.

Lastly, I think, despite being a recognized response, such a feeling originates in our deep-seated fear of the unknown. Perhaps it is a primal thing—when our ancestors looked out into the dark beyond the light of their tribal fires or community lanterns and heard the movements and howls of unknown animals, it provoked a reaction in them. Not exactly *fear* (although fear is a part of it), but some feeling that was a mixture of curiosity, anticipation, and alarm. What sort of creature waited out there in the gloom, making these noises? Once again, imagination kicked in. All sorts of bizarre creatures might lurk in the dark, and they might have glimpsed them in their mind's eye. Such things may have been spectral or unworldly, or they might have been based on creatures that they knew, distorted by the dark or failing light. Indeed, they may have recognized the calls—after all they may have seen such animals in daylight—but the darkness and the strangeness of the landscape (the *context* once again) added a different resonance to the sounds. And to some extent, that feeling hasn't left us and it forms the basis of the creepy feeling along our collective spines. This may be further linked to a feeling of helplessness in the face of an unknown danger which has been a part of us down through the ages until the present day. It even manifests itself when we watch something horrible rise up behind the hero of a film who doesn't really realize that it's there—he or she doesn't *know* where the thing is, although we do—and we're not sure what's going to happen. The feeling of "creepiness" (that awful sense of anticipation) runs through our bodies. It's the not knowing or not being in control that stimulates it.

All these factors, of course, vary from person to person, so maybe each one of you got something different out of this book. In the end, with so many other things, it is our *interpretation* that is crucial, and I hope you've found something to interpret in a way which gives you "the creeps." However, as I said, I could have filled another volume with similar places to stimulate you and leave you feeling uneasy.

And of course there are those—and I've certainly met a few of them—who have never experienced a creepy feeling in their lives. Are they any less sensitive than those who do? Are they any less imaginative? Maybe not—perhaps they just interpret the world slightly differently or perhaps they just refuse to respond to things that they don't know in a certain way. For them, things are "curious" or "interesting," but not really "creepy." They will require a different sort of book.

For the rest of us, however, such places will exercise a terrible fascination and still have the capacity to stimulate our imaginations and to give us that particular thrill that we call "creepiness." Long after we've closed this book, we might still have the urge to look behind the chair or in the far corners of the room. You never know what might be lurking there! Your everyday world might possibly, in some ways, be as creepy as those places that you've just read about!

Bibliography

Abbot, Henry J. *Graveyard Ghosts*. New York: Halcyon Press, 1962.

Aarneson, E. *Haunted Scandinavia*. Norway: Elsberg Press, 1968.

Blake, Tarquin. *Abandoned Mansions of Ireland*. Cork, Ireland: Collins Press, 2010.

Brauen, Martin. *Dreamworld Tibet—the Western Illusion*. Thailand: Orchid Press, 2000.

Campbell, J.G. *Haunted Mansions*. Nashville, Tenn.: Lone River Press, 1993.

Deal, Tim, ed. *Northern Haunts*. Milton, N.H.: Shroud Publications, 2008.

Elwood, James W. *Caribbean Ghosts*. London and Barbados: Gilvrey and Ward, 1901.

Jones, Richard. *Haunted Houses of Britain and Ireland*. London: New Holland Press, 2005.

Gordon, Giles. *Scottish Ghost Stories*. London: Senate, 1997.

Guiley, Rosemary E & Imbrogno, Philip J. *The Vengeful Djinn*. St. Paul, Minn.: Llewellyn, 2011.

Halliday, Roy, ed. *McX—Scotland's X Files*. Edinburgh: B&W Publishing,1997.

Harper, Charles G. *Haunted Houses*. London: Cecil Palmer Ltd, 1907.

Hauk, D.W. *Haunted Places: The National Directory*. New York: Penguin,1996.

The International Directory of Haunted Places. New York: Penguin, 2000.

Holzner, Hans. *True Ghost Stories*. New York: Dorset Press, 2001.

Karl, Jason. *An Illustrated History of the Haunted World*. London: New Holland, 2007.

McFarlane, A.W. *Tales of the Coolees*. London and Delhi, Lancet, 1905.

McGregor, Col. J.G. *Foula and Some Other Islands*. Edinburgh: Cochrane & Son, 1900.

McNeil, Robert. *Ghost Tales of the African South*. Cape Town, South Africa: Parrish Publishing, 1931.

Manners, Terry. *The Man Who Was Sherlock Holmes*. London: Virgin Books, 1997.

Marsden, Simon. *Ghosthunter: A Journey Through Haunted France*. Italy: Flammarion Press, 2006.

Marsh, Mrs. O.E. *Passing Strange*. London: Dutton and Sons, 1904.

Myers, Arthur. *The Ghostly Register: Haunted Dwellings, Active Spirits*. Chicago: Contemporary Books, 1986.

Patterson, Rose. *Hauntings in Ohio*. Little Rock, Ark.: August House, 1991.

Robertson, James. *Scottish Ghost Stories*. London: Sphere, 1996.

Saal, Deepak. *Mysteries of India*. Lahore, India: Chowdray & Co, 1898.

Index

G

Galgorm Castle, 108
Gallen Head, 51
Gateway to Hell, 124
George Lawson of Rutterglen, 51
Germany, Heidelberg, 77-82
Ghost Research Society, 16
Gibson, Wilfred, 60
Goddard, Thomasina, 32-34
Golden Vale, 91
Gore Orphanage Road, 61-69
Gottfried von Aschhausen, Bishop
    Johann, 78
Great Grimpen Mire, 24
Great Karoo, South Africa, 136-141
Gregory, Adolphus, 145-146
Gregory, Noel, 146, 148
Grevens Fejde, 44
Grey Lady, the, 46-48
Grimspound, 24

H

Hapsburg Empire, 38
Harris, Lizzie Lee, 168
Hartz Mountain country, 15
Haynes, Major Thomas J., 168
Healy, Patrick, 105
Heidelberg Man, 79
Heidelberg, Germany, 77-82
Heilingenberg, 79
Hell Fire Club, 106, 108-109
Hell Hounds, 20

Henry I of England, 112
Henry I, 116
Henry, Lord Darnley, 45
Hepburn, James, 45, 72, 75
Hermitage Castle, 70-76
Hexenturm, 77-82
Himalayas, 181
Hitler, Adolf, 84, 184
Holt, Joseph, 110
Holy Trinity churchyard, 24
Homo Heidelberginsis, 79
Houska Castle, 83-88
Hungarian whore, the, 41
Hungary, Csejthe, 37-42

I

I.R.A., 96
Illinois, Chicago, 13-18
India, Delhi, 130-135
Iorgi, 38
Ipplepen, 24
Ireland,
        County Limerick, 117-122
        Dublin, 104-110
        Wexford, 98-103
Islam Shah Suri, 131
Islami Pathans, 131

J

James VI of Scotland, 72
Jordan, 149-154

V

W

About the Author

Dr Bob Curran was born in a remote area of County Down, Northern Ireland. The area in which he grew up was rich in folklore—especially the folklore of the supernatural—and this gave him an ear for and an interest in the tales and beliefs of many people. He worked a number of jobs before going to university, where he received a doctorate in child psychology. Even so, his interest in folklore and folk culture was still very much to the fore, and this prompted him to write a number of books on the subject, including *Celtic Lord and Legend*; *Vampires*; *Werewolves*; *Zombies*, and *Lost Lands, Forgotten Realms*. Having taken a degree in history, he now lectures and broadcasts on matters of historical interest, and acts as advisor to a number of influential cultural bodies in Northern Ireland. Most recently, he has been working on advisory bodies regarding cultural links between Northern Ireland and the West of Scotland. He currently lives in Northern Ireland with his wife and young family.